Learning About Participatory Approaches in Adult Literacy Education

Andrea Pheasey
Audrey Fofonoff
Deborah Morgan
Grace Malicky
Linda Keam
Mary Norton
Veronica Park

Learning About Participatory Approaches in Adult Literacy Education. Six research in practice studies. © 2000. Learning at the Centre Press

Edited by Mary Norton and Grace Malicky
Copy edited by Betty Gibbs
Desk top publishing by Phyllis Steeves
Publishing assistance by Dial Printing
Cover design by Elise Almeida, University of Alberta Graphic Design and Photographic Services
Printed in Canada by Dial Printing

Learning at the Centre Press
10116 - 105 Avenue
Edmonton, AB Canada
T5J 0K2

Telephone: 780-429-0675
FAX: 780-425-2205
learningcentre@compusmart.ab.ca

Canadian Cataloguing in Publication Data
Main entry under title: Learning about participatory approaches in adult literacy education
Includes bibliographical references.

1. Literacy programs - Alberta. I. Norton, Mary, 1949 - II. Malicky, Grace, 1944 -
LC154.3.E36L42 2000   374'.0124'0971234   C00-910594-8

Acknowledgements

This book is one outcome of the Participatory Approaches in Adult Literacy Education/Research in Practice project, sponsored by The Learning Centre Literacy Association, in collaboration with the University of Alberta Faculty of Education. The project was funded by the National Literacy Secretariat, Human Resources Development Canada, in partnership with Alberta Learning. The Faculty of Education also contributed a research grant and in-kind services.

Andrea Pheasey, Audrey Fofonoff, Deborah Morgan, Grace Malicky, Linda Keam, Mary Norton and Veronica Park were principal participants in the project and contributors to this book. A number of adult learners enrolled in literacy and upgrading programs also took part. They included: Alice, Barb, Barb L., Betty, Breanne, Calvin, Charlene, Ed, Fred, Helen, Holly, Jackie, Jenna, Joyce, Leona, Lil, Lily, Linda, Madeline, Mary, Miles, Nilda, Robert, Sharron, Stephanie, Tammy, Velma and Wanda, and 32 students who took part in various project related activities at their college.

Participants were supported by the programs where they worked and learned, including the Calgary John Howard Society; The Learning Centre Literacy Association, Edmonton; Northern Lakes College, Stony Pont Campus,Wabasca; the University of Alberta Faculty of Education; the Wetaskawin Community Learning Program; and The Write to Learn Program, Camrose.

Yvon Laberge was the evaluator for the project. Pat Campbell served as a research mentor and Margaret Hansberger provided research support for a project participant. Audrey Thomas invited and made arrangements for a panel of project participants to present at a research in practice seminar in British Columbia. Keith Anderson of Alberta Learning and Yvette Souque of the National Literacy Secretariat facilitated the grant application process and were supportive advocates of the project and of literacy research in practice.

Preface

In January, 1998, seven women adult educators embarked on a learning journey. Over the next two years, we traveled well-marked trails and charted new paths as we explored the terrains of participatory approaches and research in practice. We were equipped with a range of experiences and perspectives, which were shared, extended and challenged throughout the trip. We were accompanied by other adult learners who were enrolled in the literacy programs where we worked or had affiliation.

The vehicle for our journey was the Participatory Approaches in Adult Literacy Education/Research in Practice (PAALE/RiP) project. During the project, we worked with other learners to initiate participatory projects or extend projects that were underway. In the context of the projects, we also undertook or collaborated on research about a participatory concept. Through the research, we learned more about participatory approaches, about our teaching practices and about ourselves. As well as extending our resources for daily practice, we hope our research contributes to the growing maps of participatory approaches and research in practice.

We seven include Andrea, Audrey, Deborah, Grace, Linda, Mary and Veronica. You will meet us in one or more of the chapters that follow. There are six research reports, as well as chapters about participatory approaches, research in practice and the PAALE/RiP project itself. The book concludes with reflections on the project and a description of ongoing activities.

Table of Contents

Chapter 1

The Participatory Approaches in Adult Literacy Education/ Research in Practice Project

Mary Norton

Mary Norton

The Participatory Approaches in Adult Literacy Education/ Research in Practice Project

The Participatory Approaches in Adult Literacy Education/Research in Practice (PAALE/RiP) project was initiated in January, 1998. The project built on participatory endeavours at The Learning Centre and responded to growing interests in participatory approaches among Alberta literacy educators and learners. The project also built on emerging interest in literacy research in practice and previous collaborations between The Learning Centre and the University of Alberta.

Project Origins and Influences

When the PAALE/RiP project was initiated, the term participatory approaches referred to a range of efforts that encouraged and enabled adult learners to participate actively in their learning, programs, organizations and communities. Literacy research in practice referred to research about practice, usually undertaken with or by people teaching and learning in literacy programs.

The Learning Centre is an adult literacy and education centre in downtown Edmonton. Like most community-based literacy programs in Alberta, the Centre had been developed on a learner-centred, one-to-one tutoring model. Through undertakings such as a peer tutoring project (Norton, 1996), Centre staff, students and volunteers began to explore other participatory approaches. The program evolved so that most students took part in group learning as well as one-to-one tutoring. Several students became more active in various aspects of program operations and began to extend their participation beyond the program by attending conferences and making presentations. As a program coordinator at the Learning Centre, I saw possibilities to extend, document and research participatory approaches. I talked to the Alberta government literacy consultant, Keith Anderson, about applying to the National Literacy Secretariat[1] for funding for a participatory approaches project.

Keith encouraged me to think about how a project could include people from literacy programs across the province. Initially reluctant

[1] The National Literacy Secretariat is a department in Human Resources Development Canada. Since 1988, the NLS has funded innovative projects to develop learning materials, increase public awareness, support research, improve coordination and information sharing, and improve access to literacy programs. Alberta Learning is a partner in the national literacy program.

to expand the incubating project, my enthusiasm grew as I recalled conversations with other literacy educators and learners about desires to introduce or extend participatory approaches in their programs. To assess this interest, I consulted with nine coordinators of volunteer tutor programs during a Literacy Coordinators of Alberta meeting[2]. Coordinators' responses to a questionnaire about perspectives and ideas for taking part in the proposed project helped shape the proposal. Some of these coordinators eventually took part in the project, along with other literacy educators who became involved.

A number of developments prompted and supported the inclusion of a research in practice component in the participatory approaches project. My own interest in the concept had been seeded when I attended a policy conversation on literacy research hosted by the National Literacy Secretariat in 1996. Participants in the conversation identified a need to recognize, link and support literacy research and practice (*Policy conversation on literacy research*, 1996). I was particularly inspired by discussions about supporting literacy practitioners and learners to do research. This interest was shared by Yvon Laberge, an Edmonton-based literacy researcher and consultant who also attended the policy conversation.

Prompted by shared interest in research in practice, Yvon and I met to "imagine ways to encourage practitioner research in Alberta" (*Proceedings of the Research in Practice Seminar*, 1997, p.1). As a start, we conducted a literature review and surveyed six consultants about practitioner research in Canada. The consultations identified both an interest in research in practice and a number of potential barriers to practitioners engaging in research. These barriers included a misapprehension about the purposes and benefits of practitioner research, practitioners' uncertainties about their capacities to undertake research, and practitioners' need for support and resources to do research. The survey led to a seminar in Edmonton, in the fall, 1997[3]. Eighteen practitioners and researchers from across Canada participated, shared ideas and set some directions for research in practice.The seminar report outlined nine guiding values and principles.

Inclusion of the research in practice component in the PAALE/RiP project was facilitated through collaboration with the University of

[2]A Literacy Project Development Assistance (LPDA) grant enabled me to assess interest in the project through such activities as the meeting, follow-up telephone calls and other contacts with literacy educators. The grant also covered some salary costs for me to write the proposal. These grants are funded by Alberta Learning, through the Alberta Association for Adult Literacy

[3]The Research in Practice seminar was sponsored by The Learning Centre, in partnership with the University of Alberta Faculty of Education and the University of Alberta, Faculte´ Saint Jean. The National Literacy Secretariat provided a contract to implement the seminar.

Alberta, Faculty of Education. Grace Malicky, who was Associate Dean of Research and Graduate Studies when the project started, had a long-standing interest in adult literacy research and practice. I had been a student in courses Grace taught and she had been my PhD advisor. Later, The Learning Centre was a site for literacy research that Grace either initiated or supervised. Grace participated in planning the 1997 research in practice seminar and drafted the values and principles section for the report. She agreed to be a research facilitator for the PAALE/RiP project, and the University contributed her time. Grace also arranged for other university contributions to the project, including an on-line course and a research grant.

A project proposal was submitted to the National Literacy Secretariat in the fall, 1997, shortly after the research in practice seminar. By this time, five literacy educators, in addition to Grace and me, had confirmed their intention of participating in the project: Audrey Fofonoff, Andrea Pheasey, Deborah Morgan, Linda Keam and Veronica Park. Although I would be coordinating the project and filling some other roles, I also intended to work on a participatory project and do research about it. Grace was also involved in one of the participatory projects and a related research initiative. We all introduce ourselves in subsequent chapters.

Engaging in the Project

It was important to provide resources and support for project participants to undertake participatory projects and research initiatives. Support included an on-line course, face-to-face meetings, access to research mentors, and funding for time and expenses.

The project started in January with the course titled *Participatory practices in adult literacy education*. It was offered for graduate credit through the University of Alberta Department of Educational Policy Studies, with me as the course instructor. Course participants included the five other women who were part of the PAALE/RiP project, and four university students who had enrolled in the course. All of the course participants were coordinating or teaching in an adult literacy program. In order to apply course theory to practice, each engaged in a participatory project with learners in their programs. During the course, those involved in the PAALE/RiP project also initiated research about some aspect of their participatory project.

Course modules were accessed through a website and course readings were distributed by mail. A computer-based conferencing system was used for discussions and other communication and we had three on-site meetings. The course included six modules about participatory approaches, which I developed and facilitated. As well, Grace Malicky developed seven research in practice modules that were also accessed through the course website (see Chapter 3). While they were mainly a resource for those involved in the PAALE/RiP project, other course participants could access the research modules, and some did.

The course ended in April 1998, with presentations and discussion about the participatory projects. By this time, those involved in the PAALE/RiP project were well into, but not finished, their research. Support to complete the research was provided through one-to-one consultations with Grace or me. Pat Campbell, an Edmonton-based literacy researcher and consultant, had also been contracted to provide research support during the early months of the project.

Completing the data analysis and report writing continued over the next two years. Communication continued through the conferencing system or e-mail, as well as by phone and face-to-face. Grace and I provided feedback on written reports and a technical editor was contracted to edit reports and other chapters included in this publication. During the two-year period, we had one more group meeting, a number of us took part in presentations or workshops about the PAALE/RiP project, and three of us were able to attend a course about action research at Literacy BC's 1999 summer institute.

The project budget included funds to pay for course tuition and materials and travel costs to attend meetings. Participants could claim payment for up to five hours a week for time spent on research. As well, those who worked part-time could claim payment for additional time spent on facilitating a participatory project. Honoraria and expenses could also be claimed for learners who were involved in the projects.

Building on the project

As the project evolved, the research in practice gained a higher profile than the participatory approaches components. Factors which likely contributed to the increased profile included practitioners' focus on completing research reports, opportunities for practitioners to make presentations about their research, and a growing interest in research in practice in Canada. Thus, as well as contributing to experience and knowledge about participatory approaches, the project laid a foundation for promoting and supporting research in practice about adult literacy in Alberta. A project to develop a Research in Practice in Adult Literacy (RiPAL) Network was initiated in the fall, 2000.

Andrea and Veronica are participating in the new project as research mentors and this book provides some examples for new researchers.While Grace will not be playing an active role in the new project, her writing, mentoring approach and insights will provide models for the continuing work. As facilitator for the new project, I hope to incorporate learnings and insights from the PAALE/RiP project. Some of these learnings, along with findings from the project evaluation, are described in the last chapter of this book.

References

Norton, M. (1996). *Getting our own education. Peer tutoring and participatory education in an adult literacy centre.* Edmonton, AB: The Learning Centre Literacy Association.

Policy conversation on literacy research. (1996, February). Ottawa ON: National Literacy Secretariat.

Proceedings of the Research in Practice Seminar. (1997, October). Edmonton, AB.

Chapter 2

Participatory Approaches in Adult Literacy Education: Theory and Practice

Mary Norton

Learning About Participatory Approaches

Mary Norton

Participatory Approaches in Adult Literacy Education: Theory and Practice

Introduction

When colleagues ask, "What do you mean by participatory approaches?" and I give examples, they often respond with an "Aha" of recognition. Literacy educators have been practising participatory approaches in one way or another since the contemporary adult literacy field started to evolve. The term, however, has been used mainly since the late 1980s, when people in the field began to research, describe and write about learner participation.

In 1987, Paul Jurmo completed a study of learner participation practices in adult literacy efforts in the United States. He described active participation as learners having "higher degrees of control, responsibility and reward vis-à-vis program activities" (1989, p. 17). In their study of community-based literacy programs in Toronto, Gaber-Katz and Watson (1991) described learner participation as a "continuum ranging from using found materials in the program to becoming active in the community" (p. 43).

By 1989, the term *participatory literacy education* was being used to name the sorts of learner involvement that Jurmo had documented, and Fingeret (1989) described participatory education as a collaborative process that places learners at the centre of instruction. Auerbach (1993), however, distinguished between participatory education and learner-centred approaches. Auerbach described participatory education as a critical education process aimed at social change.

Jurmo's framework and Auerbach's perspective are not mutually exclusive. In fact, Jurmo included action for social change as one of the possible outcomes of learner participation practices. However, the two views do highlight the range of ways in which "participatory education" has come to be understood and used. Fingeret suggested that participatory education is both a philosophy and a set of practices. In Alberta, participatory approaches in literacy education have been shaped by an intertwining range of philosophies and practices.

The purpose of this chapter is to describe these philosophies and practices and to introduce the research that was completed through the Participatory Approaches to Adult Literacy Education/Research in Practice (PAALE/RiP) project. On the next pages you'll find an overview of philosophical influences, followed by some examples of participatory approaches in practice.

A challenge in writing the chapter is that three years have passed since the PAALE/RiP project was initiated. My understanding of participatory approaches and their roots have shifted through dialogue with others in the project, through my own research project (Chapter 8) and ongoing practice, and through the process of reading for and writing this chapter itself.

In the interest of relating philosophies and practices, I've drawn from other writers' overviews about thinking, writing and practices that span years, cultures and contexts. Recognizing the limitations of such a filtering process, I hope this chapter provides a context as you engage with the research reports in this book and reflect on your own philosophies and practices.

Participatory Approaches: Some Influences

At the start of the PAALE/RiP project, I would have named humanistic education and critical pedagogies[1] as the main influences on participatory approaches. Since then, I have come to recognize the influences of progressive education and, more particularly, of feminist pedagogies. This section includes snapshots of these educational philosophies and their influences on participatory approaches.

Progressive Education

Most closely associated with the work of John Dewey, progressive education was introduced in the early 1900s. Although Dewey focused primarily on the education of children, he was an advocate of lifelong learning and his ideas influenced adult educators (Elias and Merriam, 1995).

Progressive education challenged teacher-led, subject-centred approaches by starting with the needs and interests of the learner. Dewey believed that education could lead to social change by educating individuals in democratic values. Thus educated, individuals would in turn work for a better, democratically-based society.

Dewey's ideas lost ground after World War II, but were taken up again during the 1960s and 1970s. Whole language approaches to reading, writing and learning that were developed during that time were influenced by Dewey's ideas and by others who embraced progressive education.

[1]Historically, the term pedagogy has been defined as the science and/or art of *teaching*. Knowles differentiated between androgogy, defined as the "art and science of helping adults learn" and pedagogy, or "the education of children" (Elias and Merriam, 1995, p. 131). Tisdell (2000) defines pedagogy in terms of teaching and learning processes or interactions. Others, such as McLaren (1998) explain pedagogy in terms of educational practices and the cultural politics that such practices support.

Progressive education concepts that are reflected in participatory approaches include learner-centredness, experience-based and life-wide learning, and a reciprocal learning relationship between teachers and learners. In such a relationship a teacher is a guide and resource, rather than transmitter of knowledge. Dewey's emphasis on democracy and social change are also reflected in some participatory approaches.

Humanistic Education

Humanistic education flows from a long history but is more recently influenced by educational psychologists Maslow and Rogers and adult educator Knowles. Humanistic philosophy has had a strong influence on both general and adult education since the mid-1900s. The goal of humanistic education is "the development of persons . . . who are open to change and continued learning, . . . who strive for self-actualization, and . . . who can live together as fully-functioning individuals"(Elias and Merriam, 1995, p. 122). Humanistic education is concerned with the development of whole persons. It is believed that the betterment of individuals will lead to betterment of society as a whole.

As with progressive education, concepts of humanistic education that are reflected in participatory approaches include learner-centrednesss, experience-based and cooperative group learning and a reciprocal teaching-learning relationship. Humanistic education has also influenced participatory approaches by emphasizing self-directed learning and the development of individuals' affective and emotional, as well as cognitive, dimensions. Quigley (1997) suggests that humanism is the prevailing philosophy in adult literacy education efforts that work from learner-centred approaches, value the development of self-esteem and advocate personal or individual empowerment.

Critical Pedagogy

The terms critical, liberatory, and transformational are all used to name educational perspectives concerned with social change. In the contemporary adult literacy field, critical pedagogy is most commonly associated with the work and writing of Paulo Freire (Auerbach, 1993; Sauvé, 1987).

As a literacy teacher in Brazil in the 1950s, Freire found that the assigned primers and teaching methods were of little interest to the students—men and women who lived in slums or laboured for landholders. Freire set the assigned resources aside, encouraged people to talk about their problematic issues, and used methods such as problem posing to promote discussion and understanding about the social roots of problems and how to initiate change. The discussions also provided a context to learn reading and writing skills. Learning to "read the word" was thus contextualized in "reading the world" (Freire and Macedo, 1987).

Critical pedagogy is based in an understanding that power is unequally distributed in society and that power distribution is maintained not only by groups and institutions, but by prevailing assumptions, values and attitudes. These assumptions and values are inculcated and assimilated from early childhood on. To some extent, existing inequities are maintained because individuals and groups, including those with less power, operate according to prevailing assumptions. Reflecting the context of Brazil at the time, Freire's early work focused on class and economic structures.

Critical pedagogy starts with and values participants' knowledge of a topic or issue. It encourages teachers and learners to question and analyse prevailing systems and assumptions related to the issue, with a view to change. Change, or transformation, may include personal change for individuals. However action for social change is the goal of participatory literacy education based in Freire's work. Critical pedagogy also acknowledges that a teacher has authority, but that this should stem from knowledge and experience rather than from the teacher's position.

The influence of critical pedagogy is most obvious in participatory approaches modelled on Freirien and popular education processes. Critical perspectives have also influenced participatory approaches aimed at changing power relations and increasing learners' collective ownership, responsibility and control in literacy programs and organizations. Some researchers argue that participatory approaches create safe spaces for learners to speak up and be heard—to have influence—as a rehearsal for speaking up in other contexts (Campbell, 1994; Fingeret, 1991).

Feminist Pedagogies

Contemporary feminist pedagogies have evolved since the 1960s along with the women's movement and the development of feminist theories, including post structural and postmodern theories. Although they centre on women's experience, knowledge and needs, feminist pedagogies are not for women only. Feminist pedagogies can be described in terms of psychological and liberatory models (Grace and Gouthro, 2000; Tisdell, 2000).[2]

Psychological models focus on women's experiences and knowledge and ways women's learning may be facilitated. As in humanistic education, psychological models advocate a sharing of authority among teachers and learners. They aim to create safe spaces where women can connect with each other, gain voice and develop as individuals.[3]

Liberatory models are concerned with personal *and* social change. Although strongly influenced by Freire's work, some feminist educators critiqued his early work for inattention to structural issues of gender and race (Weiller, 1991). Liberatory feminist pedagogies are concerned with how gender, race, class and other structures intersect. They focus on the connections between individuals and these intersecting structures, rather than on the structures alone (Tisdell, 2000). Teachers are encouraged to acknowledge and examine how their identities and positions affect their authority and their relations with learners.

In practice, liberatory models encourage learners to examine how intersecting social structures have influenced their identities. Through this process, identities may change. Learners may increase their capacities to control their lives and develop new ways of acting in the world. This may include joining with others in social change efforts. Although social change is a goal of liberatory feminist pedagogies, Tisdell (2000) suggests that such changes may not be apparent within the educational setting. They may be manifested elsewhere.

As with psychological models, feminist liberatory pedagogies consider connections, rather than separations, between affective and cognitive aspects of learning and knowing. They also suggest that people develop their own versions of truth and reality, based on life experiences and positions. They encourage the telling and sharing of stories and reflection about them, and their aim is to create spaces where learners from marginalized groups can gain their voices and create new knowledge. Some liberatory feminist educators have been less concerned with creating safe spaces than in encouraging learners to find their voices as critical thinkers. For instance, hooks (1989)

---

[2]Tisdell (2000) and Grace and Gouthro (2000) differentiate between structural or liberatory models and post-structural/postmodern or positional pedagogies. For purposes of this chapter, I use the term liberatory to include the later theories and practices.

[3]*Women's ways of knowing* by Belenky, Clinchy, Goldberger and Tarule (1986) is an often-cited reference about what facilitates women's psychological development.

advocated that women work at gaining voice in situations where they may feel afraid or at risk.

Feminist pedagogies are reflected in some participatory approaches or in research about them. Gaining voice is a theme in participatory approaches and the idea of creating safe spaces where women can achieve this is reflected in the formation of women's groups and other women-positive approaches in literacy work (Lloyd, 1994). Examination of gender, other identity issues and power relations has also been introduced in some participatory education programs.

Participatory Approaches in Practice

The terms student, learner and participant are used interchangeably in this section to refer to adults involved in literacy and ABE programs.

This section describes some participatory approaches that have evolved in English-speaking Canada, including learner-centred approaches, learner involvement activities and critical and feminist participatory education.

Learner-centred Approaches

Learner-centred approaches have been a central theme in adult literacy programming in Canada, particularly in one-to-one tutoring and other community-based programs. Gaber-Katz and Watson (1991) described learner-centredness as a "process whereby learners will be involved in setting their own learning goals and determining their own curriculum" (p. 8).

Resources published since the 1980s have encouraged tutors to develop lessons that relate to learners' interests and goals (*It works both ways*, 1983; *Journeyworkers*, 1986; Cameron and Rabinowitz, 1988; Campbell and Brokop, 1997). As noted in an early resource,

> Teaching in context means using materials that have meaning for your students. Materials that interest them provide a motivation for reading and also allow them to use what they already know to get meaning from what they want to read. (*It works both ways*, 1983, p. 26)

Jurmo (1989) found that learning is more successful when learners have opportunities to take active roles in creating meaningful materials for themselves and others. He also described how learner-centred approaches lead to enhanced personal development when learners set their own goals and identify and use resources and strategies to meet them. In these ways, learner-centred approaches support cognitive and affective development.

Learner-centred approaches also emphasize equality among learners and teachers or tutors (Gaber-Katz and Watson, 1991; Fingeret, 1990). However, experiences and assumptions about traditional teacher-student power relations can make it difficult to shift to more egalitarian approaches. Rodriguez argued that implementing learner-centred approaches required teachers and learners to examine the "fundamental relationship between instructors and students" (*Student-centred learning*, 1989).

Auerbach (1993) welcomed the shift from approaches based in predetermined or teacher-directed curriculum to learner centredness. However, from a critical pedagogy perspective, she summarized a number of concerns about learner-centred approaches. She argued that learner-centred curriculum, with its focus on individual interests, will not likely lead to social analysis. Gaber-Katz and Watson (1991) also questioned

> whether a self-determined curriculum, which focuses on the individual learner's experience, can also be a "social change" curriculum that will support the empowerment of individuals and the community through collective action. (p. 27)

Learner-centred approaches have also been challenged for their focus on individual tutoring or learning. Although learner-centred tutoring encourages students to have active roles in their learning, group contexts provide for learning with others who have had common experiences. Participatory learning in a group enables learners to share ideas, build meaning and model cognitive strategies (Jennings and Xu, 1996) and some learners prefer to learn with peers (Gaber-Katz and Watson, 1991). According to Rodriguez, learner-centred approaches do not

> necessarily mean separating individuals and reinforcing their sense of isolation. On the contrary, student-centred learning means respecting the individual's needs and background while recognizing the power, supportiveness and common issues of the group. (*Student-centred learning*, 1989)

Tremblay and Taylor (1998) found that Aboriginal learners in an employment preparation program valued the learner-centred and co-operative, interactive dimensions of the program and suggested that these approaches could be applied with other groups of learners.

Learner-centred approaches, whether applied in one-to-one tutoring or groups, often reflect progressive and humanistic perspectives. However, they can be starting points for participatory education based in critical and feminist pedagogies.

Learner Involvement in Programs and Organizations

The terms "learner involvement" and "learner participation" have been used to express similar meanings in Canada.

As introduced by Jurmo (1989), participatory education includes learner participation in a range of program activities. Campbell (1994) defined participatory literacy practices as "the active involvement of students in the operation of one or more components of their adult literacy program" (p. 127).

In Canada, learner involvement in organizations has evolved at local, provincial, territorial and national levels. In programs, learner involvement has included serving on boards, assisting with program operations and fund raising, speaking to the media, participating in tutor training, forming student groups, and peer tutoring (Campbell, 1994; Gaber-Katz and Watson, 1991; Goldgrab, 1992; Norton, 1992, 1996; Williams and Knutson-Shaw, nd).

Serving on boards and committees has been a main focus of learner involvement in national, provincial and territorial organizations. In the late 1980s, the Movement for Canadian Literacy (MCL) adopted a position of promoting student/learner representation on boards of literacy organizations. The Learners Action Group of Canada (LAGOC) was formed to advocate for and support student organizing. In 1990, the group hosted a training event to prepare learners from across Canada for leadership roles. One outcome of the event was a mission statement aimed at laying a foundation for strengthening the voice of adult students. The statement advocated

> that the 50/50 partnership for student /learner involvement existing in 1-to-1 tutoring be extended by 1995 to include all levels of literacy organizations including programs, boards and networks. . . . (*National learners training event*, 1990)

In response to LAGOC efforts, a learner involvement committee was formed in Alberta, under the umbrella of the Alberta Association for Adult Literacy (AAAL). The committee organized a leadership training event (*Building the network*, 1992) and gained learner representation on the AAAL board. Since 1990, the AAAL has provided funding for learners to attend the annual literacy conference.

By the early 1990s, learner representatives were serving on a number of provincial and territorial literacy organizations (Campbell, 1994). The principle of 50/50 partnership was implemented by the MCL board and provision was made for student representation on the board from each province and territory.

In 1997, the MCL adopted a revised constitution that provided for a Learners' Committee with representation on the Board. Echoing the 1990 mission statement, the Learners' Committee has a mandate "to work with the Board towards the goal of strengthening the adult student/learner voice in Canada" (Movement for Canadian Literacy, 1997). This includes developing leadership skills of learner board members and building links between MCL and learner networks.

Reports by learner committee members point to a variety of ways in which they and other learners are involved at provincial levels (*Learners in Action*, 1998, 2000). These include attending forums and conferences, speaking at events, meeting with politicians and representing learners on coalition boards. There are learner networks in at least five provinces. In British Columbia, the Learners Educational Action Research Network did research about building connections among learners in the province (*Action research*, in press).

Research has identified various benefits to learner involvement in programs and organizations (Blais, 1992; Campbell, 1994; Jurmo, 1989; Norton, 1992, 1996). Personal development, increased confidence and renewed self-esteem are recurring themes. Being part of a community, developing personal relationships, sharing knowledge and helping others were also identified as benefits. The themes of having a voice and sharing power also recur in the research about learner participation.

In her chapter on research in practice in this book, Grace Malicky makes a distinction between participation (to share or take part) and involvement (to include). Learner involvement has been encouraged with the intention of participation, but less active involvement has sometimes been the result. As Campbell (1992) noted, serving on program boards may take the form of involvement or more active participation, depending on the extent to which ownership and power is shared.

With their emphasis on student-teacher equality, learner-centred and learner-involvement approaches may address power and authority issues that are inherent in teacher-student relationships. However, such changes do not necessarily confront contradictions that arise from differences in race, gender, class background, income and the like (Lloyd, 1994). Based on her research about participatory practices in student groups, Campbell (1996) argued for recognizing and working across identity differences among students as well as between students and teachers. Working with differences also challenges the idea of a unitary student voice and makes space for a range of voices.

Campbell (1994) argued that "systemic factors . . . play a significant role in silencing people" (p. 72) and suggested that student groups can provide safe places for students to move from silence into speech. From a critical pedagogy perspective, changes in classroom, program and organizational power-relations are not ends in themselves. Rather, they are seen as rehearsals for changing power relations in the larger community (Auerbach, 1993; Campbell, 1994; Jurmo, 1989).

Critical Participatory Education

For some literacy educators, participatory education is a process of critical pedagogy, based in popular education models. In the mid-1980s, Arnold, Barndt and Burke (1985) wrote about their experiences of popular education in Latin America and Canada. Although not focusing on literacy in particular, their work, along with that of other popular educators, has had an influence on critical participatory literacy education in Canada.[4] Feminist pedagogies are also reflected in some of the examples that follow.

Sauvé's (1987) account of participatory education is based in a program she developed in Edmonton, starting in 1985. Through the program, women who lived with low incomes were to develop skills and access information and other supports to gain employment. As well, they were to become more skilled as consumers and more critically aware of broader consumer issues. Sauvé described how

> for two hours each Thursday morning . . . [women] gathered in the upstairs room of an Edmonton Housing Authority house to share and learn together . . . share their stories, their problems, and their dreams and help one another to address their everyday needs while at the same time learning to access the community resources they require to make their lives easier and fuller. (p. 68)

[4]Popular education has a Canadian history as well. Examples include the Antigonish Movement in Nova Scotia (Alexander, 1997) and community development movements in Quebec (Chené and Chervin, 1991). Popular education with a literacy focus has been part of the Quebec context since the 1970s.

Within the context of the program purposes, Sauvé's role included helping women to identify what and how they wanted to learn. Sauvé advocated that taking control of learning in one context brings people closer to taking control of their lives in general. The program laid the foundation for other women from the area to engage in further participatory learning and action (Scott and Schmitt-Boshnick, 1996).

In 1986, a group of women in the Winnipeg Journeys program drew together around common experiences of living with the welfare system (Norton, 1992). A facilitator from a local popular theatre organization helped the women identify and clarify issues and questions about welfare. Often questions were answered in the group but when additional information was needed, the women did research and reported back. Equipped with extended knowledge, the women took action to address problems, such as access to special needs allowances and social workers' unscheduled home visits.

Working together, the Journeys women developed a better understanding of the welfare system and gained confidence needed to speak up with social workers. To inform others and raise awareness about welfare issues, they decided to write a play, which they performed 24 times to audiences totalling 1300 people. The play was also published (The No Name Brand Clan and Lester, T., 1990). Gaber-Katz and Horsman (1990) advocate that it is "a transformative act to document learners' lives . . . and bring them into the public realm" (p. 22).

Informing others and raising awareness about discrimination was an impetus for the The Samaritan House Participatory Action Research (PAR) Group in Brandon, Manitoba. The PAR Group (1995) described participatory action research as "a way of finding out how ordinary people experience a problem or problems in their own lives and how they can take action for change" (p. 2). The group members shared their own and others' experiences of discrimination, analysed their common experiences, and planned action for change. They felt that writing a book was the best "way for us to speak up for ourselves" (p. 12).

It is noteworthy that all of these examples involved women and centred on women's experiences. This suggests that the projects reflected feminist as well as critical pedagogies, although feminist pedagogies were not named as influences. The following section includes examples of projects that drew explicitly from feminist as well as critical pedagogies.

Feminist Participatory Education

The Canadian Congress for Learning Opportunities for Women was founded in 1979 to advocate for educational policies, programs and practices that meet the needs of women. In 1990 the literacy committee of CCLOW initiated a research project about women's experiences in literacy programs (Lloyd, 1991).

In a follow-up action research project, women-positive activities were planned and carried out in literacy programs across Canada (Lloyd, 1994). The research process itself was participatory and feminist, and activities that were developed included participatory elements. For example, a woman's group was formed in the Saint John's Learning Exchange. Building on the program's learner-centred approach, the group talked about women's interests and issues, learned about themselves and supported each other. Sharing and support were also outcomes for the Beat the Street Women's Committee in Toronto. As well, this committee did research and took action to address issues of sexual harassment in their program. Their efforts led to changes that made the program safer for women.

The CCLOW action research project led to a number of recommendations for women-positive literacy work in Canada. As well, it identified a desire for curriculum material that addressed issues in women's lives, including issues of violence. This led to a curriculum development project that involved women literacy workers and learners from a variety of settings across Canada (*Making connections*, 1996).

As with the action research project, the curriculum development process was participatory and the curriculum material incorporates elements associated with participatory approaches. The curriculum is "learner-centred and respectful of differences . . . it offers learners lots of options and invites them to bring their own lives and needs into the classroom" (Nonesuch, 1996). It is also intentional about addressing issues of diversity and power, about creating knowledge and encouraging women to speak, share experiences, form alliances and work for change at personal and political levels.

Health was the focus of a participatory literacy education program with women in Edmonton. Influenced by critical and feminist pedagogies, Pat Campbell and I (Norton and Campbell, 1998) used a popular education process developed by Arnold and his colleagues (Arnold et al., 1991) and encouraged women to analyse health issues in terms of gender structures.

We came to understand participatory education as involving people in

> ... learning, building knowledge and taking action about topics and issues that matter to them. A vision of participatory education is that people can make things better for themselves, their families and their communities. (p. 8)

Evaluation research about the project indicated that women did make some changes for themselves. However, one of the greatest benefits that women reported was being able to meet and talk openly with other women.

Reflecting about the project, we realized that although we invited analysis of gender as well as economic structures, the project did not invite examination of race, culture or other factors. Although participants included Aboriginal and non-Aboriginal women, there was little attention in the project to traditional Aboriginal health practices or to the identities of women in matriarchal Aboriginal societies.

Women's journeys in self-discovery was a project sponsored by the Edmonton John Howard Society and Elizabeth Fry Society of Edmonton (Murphy and Sochatsky, 2000). Feminist and participatory education principles guided project development through four cycles. In each cycle a facilitator worked with a group of women in either a correctional institution or in one of the sponsoring agencies.

Early in the project, Aboriginal participants identified a desire to incorporate spiritual dimensions into their learning. In one setting, a First Nations participant facilitated a smudge to start each day's gathering. In another, some women prepared for and took part in a sweat ceremony. In evaluating the project, Aboriginal and non-Aboriginal women spoke of the importance of the spiritual dimensions of the program.

Aboriginal literacy education incorporates cultural knowledge (Akiwenzie-Damm & Halonen, n.d.), and spiritual growth is a foundation of aboriginal literacy (National Aboriginal Design Committee, 2000; Orr, 2000). Participatory approaches, particularly those based in feminist pedagogies, can include sharing and learning from cultural and spiritual perspectives.

Learning about Participatory Approaches

As the coordinator for the Participatory Approaches in Adult Literacy Education (PAALE/RiP) project, one of my roles was to develop and facilitate an interactive, computer-based course about participatory approaches. Course participants included the five women whose research reports are published in this book and four other women. During the three-month course, we engaged in reading, discussion and reflection about philosophy and practices in participatory approaches. In developing the course, I tried to use a critical participatory education model developed by Arnold et al. (1991).

We started the course by pooling and debating our ideas, experiences and visions about participatory approaches. This initiation was followed by an exploration of related literature. We extended our knowledge as we compared perspectives presented in the literature with our own views. Resources for practice were also among our readings as we began to implement participatory projects in our own settings. By this time, those of us in the PAALE/RiP project were also starting our research, drawing on the resources that Grace Malicky describes in the next chapter. Grace was the research facilitator for the project.

The projects and research described in the reports in this book reflect the authors' understanding of participatory approaches and the range of perspectives and practices that have influenced the adult literacy field. Audrey Fofonoff drew on her beliefs and experiences with learner-centred approaches as she found and used culturally relevant reading and writing resources. Her research goal was to determine whether a series of theme-related activities incorporating listening, observing, writing, reading and questioning/discussion skills would enhance students' knowledge about the encompassing theme of Cree culture and lifestyle. Audrey was also interested in relinquishing her "habitual leadership role in the classroom at appropriate times to allow students' voices to strengthen within our classroom groups and possibly beyond in the community" (Fofonoff, p.78, this volume).

The program where Linda Keam works encourages adult learners to take active roles in framing their learning experiences, and tutors are encouraged to work closely with learners to select appropriate learning materials. Linda extended this learner-centred approach by inviting learners to solicit and select learners' writings for a curriculum resource. She undertook research about the form learner participation would take in this curriculum project and about benefits of participation.

Andrea Pheasey and Grace Malicky participated with a group of students who undertook an action research project aimed at increasing computer use in their program. Andrea also did research about how, as a group, the students were able to address and solve a problem that they could not or would not deal with as individuals.

Deborah Morgan's research also led to examination of group processes. After the conclusion of a woman's writing program that Deborah had facilitated, some of the participants decided to form a women's writing group. Deborah encouraged women in the group to share the facilitating role and she undertook research about the sharing process.

I also examined my role as a facilitator as I worked with a group of students who had decided to host a student conference. My research focused on whether and how I shared power with the group. Starting from a critical perspective, my analysis and writing drew me into feminist theory and pedagogies.

Veronica Park asked a group of adult students to help design a needs assessment to find out what kind of literacy services were needed in the community. The group, however, was adamant that the program only needed to be promoted. As a result, they planned, set up and staffed a promotional display at a local mall. As Veronica reviewed tapes of group meetings, she found that the group's discussion revealed a number of reasons why adults don't enrol in programs. Veronica recognized that it is not enough to just ask students for their input; rather, practitioners need to set aside preconceived ideas and learn to listen.

Veronica's project is an example of critical learning in practice. The students challenged both Veronica's intention to conduct a needs assessment and conventional ideas about why people don't enrol in literacy programs. Following a dialogue about their own experiences, the group initiated action to promote literacy services in ways that they thought appropriate.

The participatory projects, while not necessarily framed in terms of critical perspectives, all had to do with shifting power relations. To this extent, the projects challenged conventional ideas about teacher-learner roles in educational settings and presented alternatives for sharing power.

References

Action research. Learning how to build a provincial learner network of networks. (in press). Vancouver, BC: Literacy BC.

Akiwenzie-Damm, K., & Halonen, D. (n.d.). *Empowering the spirit. Native literacy curriculum.* Owen Sound, ON: Ontario Native Literacy Coalition.

Alexander, A. M. (1997). *The Antigonish Movement. Moses Coady and adult education today.* Toronto, ON: Thompson Educational.

Arnold, R., Barndt, D., & Burke, B. (1985). *A new weave. Popular education in Canada and Central America.* Toronto, ON: Canadian University Services Overseas Development Education and Ontario Institute for Studies in Education.

Arnold, R., Burke, B., James, C., Martin, D., & Thomas, B. (1991). *Educating for a change.* Toronto, ON: Between the Lines and the Doris Marshall Institute for Education and Action.

Auerbach, E. (1993). Putting the P back in participatory. *TESOL Quarterly, 27,* 543-45.

Belenky, M. F., Clinchy, B. M., Goldberger, N. R., & Tarule, J. M. (1986). *Women's ways of knowing.* Stockbridge, MA: Basic Books.

Blais, H. (1992). Dialogue with decision makers. In J. Draper & M. Taylor (Eds.), *Voices from the literacy field* (pp. 219-229). Toronto, ON: Culture Concepts.

Building the network, learning to lead. A workshop for adults in literacy and adult basic education programs. (1992). Calgary, AB: The Alberta Association for Adult Literacy.

Campbell, P. (1992). The experiences of student board members in an adult literacy program. Unpublished paper. (ERIC Document Reproduction Services No. ED 401 393)

Campbell, P. (1994). *Participatory literacy practices. Having a voice, having a vote.* Unpublished doctoral dissertation, University of Toronto, Toronto.

Campbell, P. (1996). Participatory literacy practices: Exploring social identity and relations. *Adult Basic Education, 6,* 127-142.

Campbell, P., & Brokop, F. (1997). *Staple '96 [computer file]: Supplemental training for Alberta practitioners in literacy education*. Calgary, AB: Literacy Coordinators of Alberta.

Cameron, J. & Rabinowitz, M. (1988). *A guide for tutoring adult literacy students*. Victoria, BC: Ministry of Advanced Education and Job Training.

Chené, A., & Chervin, M. (1991). *Popular education in Quebec. Strengthening social movements*. Washington, DC: American Association for Adult and Continuing Education.

Elias, J. L., & Merriam, S. B. (1995). *Philosophical foundations of adult education* (2nd ed.). Malabar, FL: Kreiger.

Fingeret, A. (1989). The social and historical context of participatory literacy education. *New Directions for Continuing Education, 42*, 5-15.

Fingeret, H. A. (1990). Changing literacy instruction. Moving beyond the status quo. In F. P. Chisman (Ed.), *Leadership for literacy. The agenda for the 1990's* (pp. 25-50). San Francisco: Jossey-Bass.

Fingeret, H. A. (1991). Meaning, experience and literacy. *Adult Basic Education*, (1),4-11.

Freire, P. & Macedo, D. (1987). *Reading the word and the world*. South Hadley, MA: Begin and Garvey.

Gaber-Katz, E., & Horsman, J. (1990). Is it her voice if she speaks her words? *Voices Rising, 4*(1), 22.

Gaber-Katz, E., & Watson, G. M. (1991). *The land that we dream of. A participatory study of community-based literacy*. Toronto, ON: OISE.

Goldgrab, S. (1992). Activating student participation. In J. Draper, & M.Taylor (Eds.), *Voices from the literacy field* (pp. 231-242). Toronto, ON: Culture Concepts.

Grace, A. P., & Gouthro, P. A. (2000). Using models of feminist pedagogies to think about issues and directions in graduate education for women students. *Studies in continuing education, 22*(1), 5-28.

hooks, b. (1989). *Talking back. Thinking feminist. Thinking black*. Boston: South End Press.

It works both ways. Teaching reading and writing to adults. (1983). Edmonton, AB: ACCESS Alberta.

Jennings, C. M., & Xu, D. (1996). Collaborative learning and thinking. The Vygotskian approach. In L. Dixon-Kraus (Ed.), *Vygotsky in the classroom. Mediated literacy instruction and assessment* (pp.77-92). White Plains, NY: Longman.

Journeyworkers. Approaches to literacy education with adults. (1988). Calgary, AB: ACCESS Network.

Jurmo, P. (1989). The case for participatory literacy education. *New Directions for Continuing Education, 42,* 17-34.

Learners in action. (1998). Ottawa, ON: Movement for Canadian Literacy.

Learners in action. (2000). Ottawa, ON: Movement for Canadian Literacy.

Lloyd, B. A. (1991). *Discovering the strength of our voices. Women and literacy programs.* Toronto, ON: Canadian Congress for Learning Opportunities for Women.

Lloyd, B. A. (1994). *Women in literacy speak. The power of women-positive literacy work.* Toronto, ON: Canadian Congress for Learning Opportunities for Women.

Making connections. Literacy and EAL curriculum from a feminist perspective. (1996). Toronto, ON: Canadian Congress for Learning Opportunities for Women.

McLaren, P. (1998). *Life in schools. An introduction to critical pedagogy in the foundations of education.* (3rd ed.). New York: Longman.

Movement for Canadian Literacy. Constitution and bylaws. (March, 1997). [On-line] Available: http://www.literacy.ca/about /conby/ cover.htm

Murphy, J. & Sochatsky, B. (2000). *Women's journeys in self-discovery. An integrated literacy and lifeskills approach to literacy.* Edmonton, AB: Edmonton John Howard Society and the Elizabeth Fry Society of Edmonton.

National Aboriginal Design Committee. (2000). [video recording].

The No Name Brand Clan, & Lester, T. (1990). *Under the line. A witty down to earth look at life on welfare.* Winnipeg, MB: Popular Theatre Alliance.

Nonesuch. K. (1996). What is a feminist curriculum? In *Making connections. Literacy and EAL curriculum from a feminist perspective* (pp. 9-14). Toronto, ON: Canadian Congress for Learning Opportunities for Women.

Norton, M. (1992). Literacy, welfare and popular education. In J. Draper & M. Taylor (Eds.), *Voices from the literacy field* (pp. 103-112). Toronto, ON: Culture Concepts.

Norton, M. (1992). Sharing power and authority. In J. Draper & M. Taylor (Eds.), *Voices from the literacy field* (pp. 195-204). Toronto, ON: Culture Concepts.

Norton, M. (1996). *Getting our own education. Learning about participatory education in an adult learning centre*. Edmonton, AB: The Learning Centre Literacy Association.

Norton, M. & Campbell, P. (1998). *Learning for our health: A resource for participatory literacy and health education with women*. Edmonton, AB: The Learning Centre Literacy Association.

Orr, J. A. (2000). Learning from Native adult education. In L. M. English & M. A. Ilen (Eds.), *Dimensions of adult learning. What educators can do* (pp. 59-65). San Francisco: Jossey-Bass.

Quigley, A. (1997). *Rethinking literacy education. The critical need for practice-based change*. San Francisco: Jossey-Bass.

Samaritan House PAR Group. (1995). *Where there is life there is hope. Women literacy students and discrimination*. Brandon, MB: Literacy and Continuing Education Branch, Department of Education and Training.

Scott, S., & Schmitt-Boshnick, M. (1996). Collective action for women in community-based program planning. *New Directions for Adult and Continuing Education, 69*, 69-79.

Sauvé, V. (1987). *From one educator to another. A window on participatory education*. Edmonton, AB: Grant MacEwan Community College.

Student-centred learning. (1989). [Video recording]. (Effective instruction of Native adults). Victoria, BC: Learning Resources Branch.

Tisdell, E. (2000). Feminist pedagogies. In E. Hayes & D. D. Flannery (Eds.), *Women as learners. The significance of gender in adult learning*. San Francisco: Jossey-Bass.

Tremblay, P. C. & Taylor, M. C. (1998). Native learners' perceptions of educational climate in a Native employment program. *Adult Basic Education, 8*(1), 30-46.

Weiller, K. (1991). Friere and a pedagogy of difference. *Harvard Educational Review, 61*(4), 449-474.

Williams, C. & Knutson-Shaw, B. (n.d.). *Learners as leaders. A manual for student involvement*. Vulcan, AB: The Write Break Adult Literacy Project.

Chapter 3

Research in Practice

Grace Malicky

Grace Malicky

Research in Practice

Grace Malicky

Some of the other terms in the literature include action research, teacher research, participatory research, participatory inquiry, action inquiry, and collaborative inquiry (Deshler and Ewert, 1995). We first used the term research in practice as the focus of a seminar held in Edmonton in October 1997. Eighteen participants from across Canada shared information and generated possibilities for research in practice at this seminar.

Mary Norton and I chose the term *research in practice* very deliberately for this project. The word *practice* explicitly designates that the focus of our research is on what happens in literacy programs. Even more significant is the word *in*. Research has traditionally been conducted *on* practice by someone outside of the instructional context, often a university-based faculty member or graduate student. In contrast, research *in* practice is conducted by insiders—instructors, learners, volunteers and tutors. So what is an academic like me doing in a project on research in practice?

I had been a university faculty member for 25 years at the time I became involved in this project. I had conducted research *on* adult literacy since the late 1970s and taught the first course offered at the University of Alberta on adult literacy in the 1980s. Mary Norton was a student in that course, and I have continued to work with her in a variety of ways ever since. By the early 1990s it had become clear to me that literacy is at least as much a socio-political phenomenon as it is educational (Malicky, 1991), and I was becoming increasingly skeptical regarding the usefulness of my research *on* adult literacy. Hence, when Mary asked me if I would like to work with her on the participatory approaches project reported in this book, I accepted her invitation with enthusiasm. Making the shift from research *on* practice to research *in* practice, however, was not always easy. But before I share some of the challenges of research in practice, I begin with a consideration of two dichotomies and their implications for research.

Researchers v. Practitioners

A dichotomy is the division of something into two parts. Some dichotomies, such as quantitative v. qualitative, are used to differentiate research on the basis of underlying assumptions regarding the nature of knowledge and of how research is conducted. Other dichotomies distinguish individuals who do research from those who do not. One of these, researchers v. practitioners, is commonly used to differentiate between academics in higher education contexts and educators in the field. One implication of this dichotomy is that academics are not practitioners, but this is clearly not the case. Both academics in universities and practitioners in other adult education contexts, including adult literacy programs, engage in the practice of teaching adults. We are all teachers. The difference is that the job description of university faculty members includes research and service *as well as* teaching, whereas this is generally not the case for practitioners in other adult education programs. There is little support and even less reward for practitioners outside of universities and colleges to engage in research activities.

One negative outcome of a dichotomy between researchers and practitioners is that "research is usually thought to be the exclusive domain of 'researchers'—distant, smart, erudite, perhaps university-based people who have the power to name what is to be known and how to know it" (Peters, 1997, p. 63). The argument is generally presented as one related to quality, with many of those inside dominant research paradigms using "established terms, conventions, standards, and definitions to evaluate, and essentially dismiss, alternative ones" (Cochran-Smith and Lytle, 1999, p. 23). However, as Quigley (1997) notes:

> The issue of research and knowledge production is a debate not simply over type of method, but over control of the research agenda of the future and who will have the authority to produce the knowledge we will use and be known for as a field of study and practice. (p. 12)

The research reported in this volume negates the view that only the minority in academia is capable of conducting high quality research. I have come to believe that thinking in daily life is not essentially different from that in academic life. Although research is more systematic than everyday thinking, everyone who can understand or reflect on education can learn to engage in this systematic process. From this perspective, practitioners and learners in the field have a significant role in the production as well as consumption of knowledge.

Another negative outcome of a dichotomy between researchers and practitioners involves a separation of theory and practice. Many practitioners in the field question the relevance of knowledge generated by academics in the "ivory tower" to their daily work. It's not so much the "consumer of information" role attributed to them by academics that they reject, but rather the information itself as being irrelevant. At the same time educational research is often criticized by academics as being too applied and not theoretical or "basic" enough (Blunt, 1994). According to Kemmis and McTaggart (1984, cited in Quigley, 1997), "Action research provides a way of working which links the theory and practice into the one whole: ideas-in-action" (p. 5). A major purpose of research in practice is to improve professional practice while at the same time increasing knowledge about curriculum, teaching and learning.

Insiders v. Outsiders

I believe that adult literacy research can and should be conducted by those engaged in the practice. Faculty members and graduate students at universities and colleges are generally outsiders, whereas instructors, tutors and learners are insiders. When academics conduct research, the research problem nearly always originates outside of programs, and instructors and learners are treated as passive objects of research. In contrast, research in practice

> seeks to break down the distinction between the researchers and the researched and the subjects and objects of knowledge production through the participation of the people-for-themselves in the attainment and creation of knowledge. (Gaventa, 1991, p. 121)

This does not mean that only research conducted by insiders is of value. Horsman and Norton (1999) argue that research in practice creates a place alongside academic research for knowledge situated in classroom practice. I would argue also that university-based researchers have a place in research in practice, but that our role is different from the one we have traditionally assumed. Although university-based researchers rarely become "real" insiders, we can conduct research *with* rather than *on* participants. Rather than the university-based researcher owning and controlling the research process, all participants in research in practice are involved in setting the agenda, collecting and analysing data, and controlling the use of outcomes. However, because each participant brings different knowledge and expertise to the process, each participates in different, yet equally valuable, ways.

One of the researchers in this project shared the following thoughts about research at a face-to-face meeting: "I assumed I couldn't understand a word they said. Now I know I can talk about it, understand the terminology. I have confidence in how I understand it. I'm not afraid of research. I used to be afraid, but now I am interested and excited" (Horsman & Norton, 1999, p. 1).

The view of research in practice presented in this book involves a change in relationships among research participants and in the roles they play. As in all participatory practices, relationships among researchers are collaborative and egalitarian rather than hierarchical, making the research process more democratic than when conducted by outsiders. Research in practice blurs the lines between those who *do* research and those who *consume* it. For both university-based and field-based researchers, this change in identity appears to be more difficult than learning how to actually do the research itself. It took considerable time for the practitioners involved in the research reported in this volume to come to view themselves as researchers. It may be even more difficult for academics to view themselves as equal members of a research team involving non-academics.

For the research reported in this volume, I assumed three different roles. As a resource person, I was involved in developing on-line units on research in practice and answering questions about research at meetings of the research in practice group. This role was similar to the one I regularly play as a university instructor.

The second role involved working as a research facilitator with individual researchers. Although I have worked in a somewhat similar way with graduate students on their research, in this context I needed to move from a supervisory to a collaborative stance. For example, Mary Norton and I decided together that it would be better to have the final interviews of members in her conference group conducted by someone other than her. Since I had attended some conference group meetings and had established some degree of familiarity with committee members, she asked me to conduct semi-structured interviews using questions she had prepared.

The third role I played in the research was as a kind of ex-officio member of the computer group involved in Andrea Pheasey's research. I attended weekly meetings and volunteered to undertake tasks that involved specialized research skills; for example, I worked with other members of the group to develop a questionnaire and collate data collected.

Although I engaged in a considerable number of hands-on research activities in this project, I make no claim that I was a "real" insider in any of the three roles described above. I had knowledge about research techniques that was useful to other participants, but they had knowledge of the context that I, as a university-based researcher, could never fully share.

A Continuum of Research in Practice

Research in practice is not a specific research method—there is no one right way to do it (Peters, 1997). Rather, it encompasses a wide range of possibilities, reflecting to a large extent the "multiple roots and many agendas it has served" (Cochran-Smith and Lytle, 1999).

The research reported in this volume falls along a continuum, ranging from practitioner research at one end, through action research somewhere in the middle, to participatory action research at the other end (*see* Figure 1). All three types of research involve participation in the sense intended by McTaggart (1991). He contrasts participation with involvement; participation means to share or take part, whereas involvement means to entangle, implicate or include. The major difference between participation and involvement relates to ownership. In all three types of research on our continuum, the research process is owned by insiders; one major difference among the three types is in how broadly this ownership is shared.

Figure 1. A Continuum of Research in Practice

Practitioner Research	Action Research	Participatory Action Research
Purpose set by practitioner	Purpose set by practitioner, often with input from group	Purpose set and research conducted by group
To increase understanding of practice	To implement educational change	To implement sociopolitical change
Focus on improvement of practice	Focus on improvement of practice	Focus on emancipation of oppressed people

In practitioner research, the research question and process primarily belong to the instructor, possibly with assistance from a research facilitator. In action research, there is generally a broader sharing of ownership but often it is still the practitioner who identifies the problem to be solved. In participatory action research, a group identifies the problem, develops a research process, and conducts the research. This group often involves learners as well as tutors and instructors. Fundamental to participatory action research is that "all participants actually do research for themselves" (McTaggart, 1991, p. 170).[1]

Another major difference among the three types of research on our continuum involves intent or purpose of the research. In practitioner research, the focus is primarily on the development of a better understanding of the nature of practice. In action research, an action is initiated to improve practice and the impact of that action is investigated. The purpose of both practitioner and action research is to close the gap between theory and practice—to "provide outcomes that have an application immediately related to the practice world of the individuals involved" (Quigley, 1997, p. 17).

In contrast, most proponents of participatory action research stress the importance of change beyond the practical, local level. Participatory action researchers "change themselves, they support others in their own efforts to change, and together they work to

[1]The importance of extending participation in research to instructors and learners is recognized in the Framework for the Research Support Activities of the National Literacy Secretariat released in February 1998.

change institutions and society" (McTaggart, 1991, p. 175). From this perspective, research is not only a means to create knowledge but a tool for developing people's consciousness of how power structures work as well as for mobilizing them for action (Gaventa, 1991). The goal of participatory action research is similar to that of critical education as described by Mary in Chapter 2. Both strive to achieve the emancipation of people from oppressive structures.

> Research is one tool for radical social change through action. . . the purpose of research is not merely to describe or uncover interpretations of social dynamics, but to do something about social contradictions and inequities. (Maguire, 1987, p. 16)

The intent is to transform reality *with* rather than *for* oppressed people. Participatory action research assumes that there is a political nature to everything that we do and that all of our work has implications for the distribution of power.

I do not mean to imply that practitioner and action research never has a broader agenda. The ultimate goal of some practitioner research is educational reform (Clandinin and Connelly, 1995; Cochran-Smith and Lytle, 1999). This requires that practitioner and action researchers not only share the findings of their research with the broader community of educators but also that they relate their findings to those of other researchers to create a new "baseline of possibilities" (*Proceedings of the Research in Practice Seminar*, 1997). A comparison of outcomes of practitioner and action research projects can suggest which new approaches are more promising than old ones and provide a basis for recommendations for change. The major focus of practitioner and action research, however, is on improvement of practice rather than on political change.

It is not surprising that each point on the continuum presented in Figure 1 has different roots. The practitioner research movement is grounded in Kindergarten to Grade 12 schooling and in teacher education programs designed to prepare teachers for this context (Cochran-Smith and Lytle, 1999). Action research can trace its roots to community and rural development (McTaggart, 1991) and more recently to teacher education (e.g., Laidlaw, 1992). Participatory action research is rooted in community development, particularly in third world countries, and in popular education (e.g., Gaventa, 1991). The Highlander Research and Education Center in Tennessee is one of the best-known sites in North America for participatory action research in addition to popular education, as Mary noted in Chapter 2.

Our Research

The research reported in this volume was conceived and conducted by literacy educators. Two of these educators had completed research as part of graduate programs; the other four did not view themselves as researchers at the beginning of the project and, indeed, had many questions regarding their ability to engage in this type of activity.

Three types of support were provided for researchers in this project. First, I developed a set of on-line units on research in practice that dealt with the following topics:

Unit 1 - Introduction to Research in Practice

Unit 2 - Getting Started: Reflecting on what we want to know and establishing relations among participants

Unit 3 - Planning: Refining the question and planning the research process

Unit 4 - Action: Doing something

Unit 5 - Observation: Collecting information

Unit 6 - Reflection: Thinking about what we learned

Unit 7 - Dissemination: Sharing what we learned

On-line readings and selected web sites focusing on practitioner, action, and participatory action research were included with these units.

The second type of support involved three face-to-face meetings in which participants in this project had an opportunity to talk about the progress they were making on their research and to ask questions. Finally, each researcher was linked with a research facilitator with whom she met individually.

In addition to conducting her own research, Mary Norton met regularly with three researchers (Deborah, Audrey and Veronica) and I met regularly with two researchers (Mary and Andrea). Pat Campbell served as facilitator for Linda at the beginning of the project but was unable to continue because of other commitments. I then provided some assistance to Linda but she also received additional help from a researcher at her local university. Mary and I both struggled with the role of facilitator in research in practice. How much structure could or should we provide without taking over ownership of the research? At times we provided less structure than many researchers wanted, for example when we decided against providing a common format for written reports. At other times we likely provided more structure than some wanted when we asked them to include references to the literature in their research reports.

The range of research presented in this volume reflects different contexts within which researchers worked, as well as differences in their concepts of participatory approaches and research in practice. In a sense, all of the research included is action research, since each researcher was actively engaged in the integration of participatory practices into her literacy program. However, two of the researchers, Mary and Deborah, focused primarily on understanding their role as facilitator within a participatory approaches framework; hence, their studies can be placed near the practitioner research end of the continuum. Although they wanted to learn how to share leadership and power as they worked with their groups, each retained ownership and control over the research itself, establishing the research question, collecting the data (with help from me in one instance) and analysing and interpreting the information collected.

Four researchers conducted studies that were close to the middle of the continuum—action research. Audrey wanted to find out if a series of activities would enhance her students' knowledge of Cree culture and lifestyle. She implemented four activities with the students and collected information using questionnaires and written stories to determine the impact of those activities. Linda and Andrea also investigated the impact of their participatory projects on learners. Linda focused on the nature and benefits of participation and Andrea on the nature and benefits of the group process. In all three of these action research studies, the researchers established the purpose, collected and analysed the data, and interpreted their findings. Although the learners were clearly participants in the participatory project being researched, they were informants rather than participants in the research process itself. In contrast, the members of Veronica's group exerted control over some aspects of the research process. Veronica began her research with a clear idea of what she wanted to accomplish (develop a needs assessment), but the members of her group redefined the problem and the research took a very different course than she initially intended. In addition to redefining the problem, the group decided what actions to take and implemented these actions, but their involvement in the research process ended there. Veronica collected, analysed and interpreted the data, and wrote the research report.

Another study, also reported in Andrea's chapter in this volume, can be placed closer to the participatory action research end of the continuum. Although Andrea's own research focused on group process, the group she worked with undertook research aimed at increasing computer usage in their learning centre. Andrea shared power and responsibility with other participants at all stages of the computer project except writing about their research for her chapter. Students established the research question, designed instruments to collect information, analysed and interpreted information, and designed, implemented and evaluated a program on the basis of the information collected. They also wrote a report about their research (Colgan and Pheasey, 2000). Although the locus of change was primarily classroom-based, some participants reported that the research also had an impact on their lives outside the classroom.

On Commonality and Diversity

As a reader of the chapters in this volume, you will likely be struck by how different each of the research reports is. Not only do studies fall at different points on the continuum in Figure 1, but the format and style of each chapter is also unique. Because research in practice is intended to empower those involved in practice to conduct their own research, Mary Norton and I felt that it was important for the voices of individual researchers to come through in their research reports. Rather than requiring researchers to reshape their ideas into a common format, this volume presents a rich mosaic reflective of the diversity that can be expected in research in practice. Still, there are some similarities both in the research conducted and in the information included in the chapters that follow.

All researchers present information relating to the following four basic stages: planning, acting, observing, and reflecting. In the planning stage, researchers (either individually or as a group) determined what question they would focus on in their research. Most began with a vague idea of what they wanted to investigate and spent considerable time clarifying and refining their research question. Researchers then decided how they would answer the question and selected ways to gather information. They all obtained informed consent from participants in their research to ensure that ethical standards for research with human subjects were met. Anonymity was problematic in those instances where project books were published in addition to research reports. Ultimately, several individuals requested and approved having their actual names used in research reports as well as in project books.

In the acting and observing stages, each researcher implemented her participatory project, collecting information as she did so to answer the research question posed. Most information gathering techniques used by the researchers in this project can be classified as qualitative in nature (e.g., interviews, field notes, research journals), but quantitative techniques were also used (e.g., questionnaires). All researchers relied upon two or more different sources of information in order to increase the trustworthiness of their findings. Most researchers gathered information themselves, although in some instances research facilitators or other participants in the research group were also involved in the data collection process.

In the final stage of the research (reflecting), researchers analysed the information they had collected, interpreted this information and wrote research reports. For most researchers, this was the most challenging part of the research process and took considerable time to complete.

Advocates of action research often recommend that it proceed in a series of spirals or cycles (McTaggart, 1991; Kuhne and Quigley, 1997). Primarily because of time limitations, the research reported in this volume tended to involve one cycle, although there were changes in how participatory approaches were implemented as research progressed. This was perhaps most obvious in Veronica's research, where a major change was made once the group assumed control of the research agenda. The cyclic nature of research in practice is evident in the final sections of Mary's and Audrey's reports, where they describe how the results of the research they completed for this project continue to influence their practice. In the next six chapters, the researchers involved in this project share both the process and results of their research. These chapters demonstrate some of the possibilities of research in practice.

References

Blunt, A. (1994). The future of adult education research. In R. Garrison (Ed.), *Research perspectives in adult education*. Malabar, FL: Krieger.

Clandinin, D. J., & Connelly, F. M. (1995). Teachers' professional knowledge landscapes: Secret, sacred, and cover stories. In F. M. Connelly & D. J. Clandinin (Eds.), *Teachers' professional knowledge landscapes* (pp. 1–15). New York: Teachers College Press.

Cochran-Smith, M., & Lytle, S. L. (1999). The teacher research movement: A decade later. *Educational Researcher, 28*(7), 15–25.

Deshler, D., & Ewert, M. (1995). Participatory action research: Traditions and major assumptions. [On-line] Available: <http://parnet.org/tools/Tools_1.cfm>.

Gaventa, J. (1991). Toward a knowledge democracy: Viewpoints on participatory research in North America. In O. Fals-Borda & M. A. Rahman (Eds.), *Action and knowledge: Breaking the monopoly with participatory action research* (pp. 121–131). New York: Apex Press.

Horsman, J., & Norton, M. (1999, February). A framework to encourage and support practitioner involvement in adult literacy research in practice in Canada. A paper prepared for the National Literacy Secretariat.

Kemmis, S., & McTaggart, R. (Eds.) (1984). The action research planner. Geelong, Australia: Deakin University Press [Cited in Quigley, B. A. (1997). The role of research in the practice of adult education. *New Directions for Adult and Continuing Education, 73*, 3–22.]

Kuhne, G. W., & Quigley, B. A. (1997). Understanding and using action research in practice settings. *New Directions for Adult and Continuing Education, 73*, 23-40.

Laidlaw, M. (1992). Action research: A guide for use in initial teacher education programmes. [On-line] Available: http://www.bath.ac.uk/~edsajw/initial.html

McTaggart, R. (1991). Principles for participatory action research. *Adult Education Quarterly, 41*(3), 168–187.

Malicky, G. (1991). Myths and assumptions of literacy education. *Alberta Journal of Educational Research, 37*(4), 333–347.

Maguire, P. (1987). *Doing participatory research: A feminist approach.* Amherst, MA: Center for International Education, University of Massachusetts.

National Literacy Secretariat (1998). *Enhancing literacy research in Canada.* Ottawa: Human Resources Development Canada.

Peters, J. M. (1997). Reflections on action research. *New Directions for Adult and Continuing Education, 73,* 63–72.

Proceedings of the Research in Practice Seminar. (1997, October). Edmonton, Alberta.

Quigley, B. A. (1997). The role of research in the practice of adult education. *New Directions for Adult and Continuing Education, 73,* 3-22.

Chapter 4

Learning About Group Process in a Participatory Action Research Project on Computer Training

Andrea Pheasey

Andrea Pheasey

Learning About Group Process in a Participatory Action Research Project on Computer Training

Introduction

According to Jurmo (1989) active learner participation in adult literacy programs enables learners to take a higher degree of control, responsibility and reward vis-à-vis program activities. Auerbach (1992) claims that both what is learned (content) and how it is learned (process) shape students' perceptions of their own possibilities and prepare them for particular ways of acting in the outside world. When I initially became involved in the Participatory Approaches/Research in Practice project, I expected to do a project on a math theme since I was facilitating the math program at The Learning Centre. However, because the project was to be participatory in nature, the decision about what to do was made by everyone who would be involved. The students who agreed to work with me did not want to focus on math, but instead wanted to do a project on computer usage at the Centre.

Also unexpected was the way this project evolved into two different but related research projects. The first was the participatory action research on how to make better use of the computers at The Learning Centre. I will describe this research using the framework provided by Quigley and Kuhne (1997).

The second research project that I did was observational and descriptive in nature. This research focused on how, as a group, the students who did the action research were able to address and solve a problem that they could not or would not deal with as individuals. I hoped to address the problem-solving ability of the group and examine how individuals within the group used new social skills outside The Learning Centre. Auerbach (1992) states, "Classroom social relations are a microcosm of social relations beyond the classroom. Making changes inside the classroom itself models a way of addressing issues and redefining roles outside the classroom" (pp. 21–22). I will describe the social/psychological stages of group development the students went through using a model by Armstrong and Yarbrough (1996). Using the students' own words, I will also describe how they felt about their newly acquired skills and how some individuals were able to use these skills outside The Learning Centre.

My Perspective on Participatory Approaches in Adult Education

> People learn best when learning starts with what they already know, builds on their strengths, engages them in the learning process, and enables them to accomplish something they want to accomplish. This is the essence of a participatory approach. (Auerbach, 1992, p. 9)

From my perspective, a participatory approach to adult basic education assumes students have full and interesting lives. Their history and their needs provide the basis of their learning. As a practitioner in literacy, my role is to continually ask the students what they need or want to learn and what they need or want to understand better. "Adult learning theory supports the view that learners must be involved in determining both the content and direction of their education" (Auerbach, 1992, p. 14).

From this perspective, traditional math curricula are largely unworkable in an adult basic education context, because they tend to be sequential, with one concept building on another. These curricula do not take into consideration the life experience and math-related knowledge of the students. For example, if a student needs to know how to calculate the 7% GST, she or he needs that particular information. There may be no need to plow sequentially through common fractions to decimals and then to percent to obtain a 7% calculation. The concept of fractions is likely already part of the student's awareness of the world.

My experience teaching adults began with volunteer work at the YMCA and at the Calgary Immigrant Women's Society (CIWS). Working at CIWS was my first exposure to participatory education. Groups of women at CIWS had very specific and immediate needs involving English reading, writing and speaking. At first they wanted me, as the teacher, to tell them what they needed to know. However, the program was clearly designed to meet the needs of the participants, not to follow a prearranged curriculum. Once these women understood they would receive a positive response to their problems, they flooded the two-hour class with questions. The program honoured these women's life experiences and acknowledged their abilities.

Introduction to The Learning Centre and How the Computer Group Came Together

The Learning Centre is a community-based adult education facility located in downtown Edmonton. A major goal of the program is to help adults develop their reading, writing and math skills. Some students work in groups according to their interest or ability levels. Some work individually with instructors or with community volunteer tutors. Others who have taken training are themselves tutoring their peers.

At the time of the project, The Learning Centre was open for instruction four days a week, with the majority of people attending in the mornings. There was a women's group on Monday afternoons, an art class on Wednesday afternoons, and reading groups and individual tutoring sessions on Tuesday and Thursday afternoons. At any given time, there were from 50 to 60 students enrolled.

When the participatory approaches project was introduced at The Learning Centre, Mary Norton, the program coordinator, and I became involved in it. We met with students at The Learning Centre to discuss the project with them. A large number of students expressed interest in becoming involved, primarily because students at The Learning Centre had positive experiences with other participatory projects and some were familiar with research. Students worked in small groups to discuss ways they were already participating in the work of The Learning Centre.

In early January of 1998 a follow-up meeting was held to identify projects we could undertake to study participatory approaches to education at the Centre. The students generated several possibilities but expressed most interest in the following two areas: computers and a student conference[1].

On January 19, I met with the group of students who expressed an interest in working on a project related to computers. Grace Malicky from the University of Alberta joined the group at this time. The discussion around the table started with the question, "What should we work on?"

---

[1]Research about the Student Conference project is reported in Chapter 8, Challenges to Sharing Power in an Adult Literacy Education Program.

Members of the group suggested the following seven topics:

Computer classes

Workshop on computers—handouts that are readable for the students

How to do it on your own or be independent on the computer

Peer tutoring on the computers

Getting involved in cataloguing books and registration of new students

Learning to do administration jobs

Computers for better writing

As the discussion progressed, each member of this developing group related a story about an unpleasant or uncomfortable experience, either to the whole group or to me privately during the break, about their involvement with computers. All of these students had had problems with computers, as their stories indicated. By the end of this meeting, the group decided to tackle a project on computer training at The Learning Centre.

Background of the Members of the Computer Group

The computer group was made up of ten students, Grace Malicky and me. A core of seven students came to the majority of the meetings held through the winter months, but some were unable to attend the two meetings held in the summer because of family or other commitments. The three other students attended meetings less often.

The students in the computer group included eight women and two men. At the time of the project, they were all involved in a morning learning group at The Learning Centre. Some participated in other activities at the Centre as well. Four of the students had a long history together, having spent their teenage years at the same school. Four had spent more than three years at the Centre and were well known to each other. Two members had attended the Centre for less than one year but were comfortable in the group.

Grace Malicky had been a faculty member at the University of Alberta since 1975. The major focus of her teaching and research was language arts and literacy education. She had worked with Mary Norton on other projects and had some familiarity with The Learning Centre.

I started working at The Learning Centre as a volunteer. Since 1993 I have been employed as the facilitator for the math program. I also facilitate one of the reading and writing learning circles. At the time of the project, I had been involved with the Centre for seven years, so I knew most of the students in the computer group.

The Purpose of the Research
The Action Research

The Learning Centre acquired its first two computers in 1990. The number of computers increased, mainly through purchases and donations, until at the time of the computer project students at the Centre had access to 12 computers. The computers were in two rooms and were used mainly for students' writing activities.

The student members of the group identified their lack of computer skills as a problem. The students felt this problem was another way in which they were isolated from the mainstream of society and they expressed concern for their futures if they did not acquire computer skills.

> *Everything is going to be computers now.* (Velma)

> *All the stores have computers now, pretty soon everything is going to be computers . . . the offices have computers now.* (Wanda)

> *When we go out to work we will have to learn more about the computers anyway.* (Betty)

The students wanted to find out how they could make more and better use of computers. They wanted to learn computer skills themselves and then teach those skills to their fellow students. The group identified the problem as how to learn more computer skills and make better use of computers in The Learning Centre.

Most students in our group had not used the computers because they felt inadequate even to ask questions. They felt they would bother the staff or other students who did have some computer training if they asked questions. They wanted to try using the computers on their own but did not feel they knew enough to begin.

> *I'm afraid to ask stupid questions. If I ask I feel I'm bugging people.* (Velma)

> *I asked ___ and she was very busy with her own thing and every second I was asking her.* (Velma)

Some students even felt that they would somehow damage the computers if they touched them.

> *I never wanted to go near them because I was scared. They were too challenging.* (Wanda)

As a facilitator at the Centre before and during the acquisition of the computers, I knew they were a concern to some students but was unaware of the magnitude of the students' concern. I was part of this problem in two ways. First, I believed the students would ask if they wanted to be taught computer skills, and second, I did not think my own computer skills were at a sufficient level to teach others.

The computer group identified several possible benefits to The Learning Centre of taking on this project. First, the writing program at the Centre would be improved if more students had computer skills. They would be able to write and edit their stories on the computers and save their writing on disks. Second, basic skills in math could be practised in an atmosphere of fun if the students could use computer math games. Third and probably the most important benefit of finding a solution to the computer usage problem, the students would feel improved self-esteem. The students would see themselves as computer literate and able to teach others a skill.

Participatory action research as defined by Quigley and Kuhne (1997) includes not only the identification of a question, data collection and analysis but also a change in practice, the action. This project, designed by the computer group, took us through all of these steps.

The Group Process Research

In addition to the participatory action research project, I also conducted research to increase understanding of how student members of the group worked to solve a problem they had not attempted to solve alone.

At The Learning Centre we view group work as contributing to the social and emotional health of learners. Although I believe that groups are beneficial for some learners, I had never systematically investigated the group process or how group work helps learners. Imel (1996) notes, "As adult educators we have undoubtedly formed theories about the use of groups and about how learning occurs in groups. [These are] known as 'theories-in-use'" (p. 91).

According to Campbell (1996) adult literacy theory and practice emphasizes the visual aspects of literacy while the oral aspects are often neglected. Group work provides a place for the oral aspect of literacy, the speaking and listening, to occur.

There is a need for more research on the use of small group learning in adult basic education. In my research I also wanted to find out if the group members felt the skills they learned from working within a group could be transferred to other situations outside the immediate group environment.

In each of the remaining sections in this chapter, except the section on Implementing the Action, I present information on both the action research and group process research.

Defining the Research and Collecting Information

The Action Research

The group chose to name its project the Computer Project. Their first meeting was on January 26, 1998. The group decided to have weekly meetings, which were held on Monday afternoons and then moved to Thursday afternoons to accommodate one person who had a DATS (Disabled Adult Transportation System) time conflict. I was the original facilitator bringing group members together, developing the agenda for the meetings, and chairing the meetings. After the first few meetings, other members took over the job of chairing because I found it difficult to take field notes at the same time as chairing meetings. The group decided to have a rotating chair and used a consensus model to assign tasks and arrive at decisions. As a member of the group, I assumed responsibility for various jobs just like every other member. Grace volunteered to work with other group members on specific tasks such as developing a research questionnaire for the group and analysing data collected from that questionnaire.

The group decided that we needed to gather information on existing computer use at The Learning Centre before we could decide what to do to increase use of the computers. We went through three steps in gathering this information.

First, the group wanted to find out who was using the computers. Some members remarked that the same few students used the computers regularly, but no one seemed to know what these people were doing with them. We decided to hang a poster beside the computers asking people who used a computer to write their name, the date, what they were doing on the computer, how long the job took and who (if anybody) helped them if they had a problem. From this informal survey, the group discovered who was using the computers and for what purpose. The group also discovered who was not using the computers.

The group then decided more information-gathering was needed and that we needed information from everyone at The Learning Centre. We decided to develop a questionnaire to ask all students why they were not using the computers, what they knew or wanted to know about the computers at the Centre, and how they would like to be taught. (This questionnaire is included in Appendix B.) We knew that most students would be unable to complete the questionnaire on their own so three members of the group met with students individually, asked them the questions and recorded their answers on record sheets.

After we had analysed information collected on the questionnaire, we realized that we still did not know who wanted to become involved in basic computer training or who would be willing to help with this basic training. The group decided to put a poster at the entrance to the Centre. On this poster, basic training was defined as learning how to turn the computer on and off, how to start a program and how to save material on a disk. Students interested in learning basic computer skills were asked to sign their names on one side of the poster, and students who felt they could help with this basic training were asked to sign on the other side. This poster, shown below, was left up for approximately two weeks.

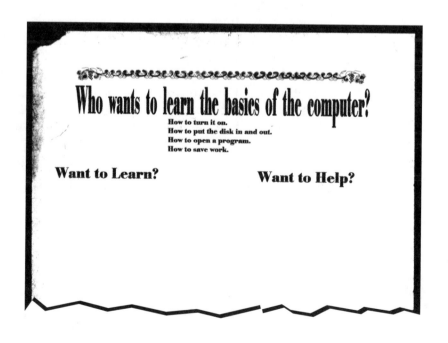

The group wanted to have the first run-through of the training and the evaluation completed before the Centre closed for the summer on June 11, 1998. We thought if the project was successful in the spring term, we could implement it again in September when the Centre reopened.

The group decided that the basic measure for determining if the project had been successful would come from observing computer use to find out if the computers were being used more at the end than at the beginning of the training program. Further, in a closing survey, the group decided to ask all students who had participated in the project, either as a trainer or trainee, if they were using the computers more at the end of the computer project. All members of the group agreed that if a majority of students at The Learning Centre stated they used the computers more after than before the training program, then the project would be a success.

In summary, data collection methods used in the action research included posters, a questionnaire, a closing survey and global observations of computer use at the Centre. Rather than asking students in the Centre to sign consent forms, we assumed consent for involvement in the research if students signed the posters and responded to the questionnaire or the closing survey.

The Group Process Research

At the beginning of the project, I used a generic permission form to obtain informed consent from student members of the computer group for participation in the group process research. This consent form confirmed that the participants agreed to be observed by me and that they could withdraw from the research at any time without penalty. As the research progressed, I realized that the consent form was inadequate because it did not refer to names, statements, pictures or video images of the students obtained during the research. A second consent form was drafted asking the students to allow me to use data collected from interviews, from their writing and from observations of the group. I also asked to use these data in written reports and conference presentations on the project. Students also consented to the use of their first names in reports.

The data collected for the group process research was in the form of field notes, tapes of interviews, and writing from group members. I interviewed the core group members once at the beginning of the planning process, once during the training phase and once at the end of term. Five members of the group agreed to be videotaped as they talked about the project at the end of the term. All interviews were transcribed.

The questions I asked in the first and second interviews are presented in Appendix A. The third interviews, which were videotaped, were more open-ended. The members were asked, "What do you feel you have learned from being in the computer group?" A discussion took place, and I asked for clarification where necessary. I transcribed the discussion and highlighted comments that pertained to my research questions.

Members of the group wrote about their experiences in the group at the end of the term in June. As with the transcripts of the interviews, I read and highlighted pertinent ideas in the writing.

Throughout the planning and training part of the project, I took field notes during meetings and edited them at the end of each meeting. These notes were used to document how the group evolved, how it approached and made decisions, how it dealt with conflict and how the members grew to understand their function within the group.

How We Analysed the Information Collected

The Action Research

Grace and Wanda collected the questionnaires, categorized and counted responses for each question and summarized the results. From these results the computer group was able to determine the priorities of the student body at The Learning Centre.

The names of those who wanted to learn more about the computers and who wanted to help with the training were collected from the poster and used to match students into training pairs. Responses on the closing survey were categorized as positive, negative and undecided, and percentages were calculated for each category.

The Group Process Research

After I transcribed the interviews, I read the transcripts and students' writing several times, highlighting the information or idea units that related to my research questions. I then placed these ideas into two categories. The first involved members' learning about themselves and others in the group. The second involved how members changed their attitudes about themselves inside and outside The Learning Centre. In particular I noted the skills the members said they had learned from the group that they could use outside The Learning Centre. I confirmed through observations and reflections in my field notes that members changed their attitudes about their ability to learn.

Planning and Implementing the Action

The Action Research

The group used results from the questionnaire and posters to plan a computer training program for students in The Learning Centre. From the results of the questionnaire the group learned that people were not using the computers because they didn't know how, they needed help or they didn't have time. Respondents to the questionnaire wanted to learn how to start and stop the computers, how to save their stories on disks, how to play games and how to make cards and posters. The majority wanted computer skills taught in a one-to-one setting. The complete results of the questionnaire are presented in Appendix C.

Results from the posters indicated that few students both had computer skills and were willing to teach other students. Early in the planning process Wanda suggested to group members that *We learn it ourselves and then teach it to others*. We needed to find someone to teach our group basic skills. The group decided to ask a community volunteer who is very knowledgeable about computers to provide training for them. The community volunteer trained two members of the group on the basics of the Macintosh computer. These two, in turn, trained the others in the group. The group thought it would be easier learning from another student because they felt they would be more comfortable asking "dumb" questions of another student. As Madeline indicated, *A student likes to be taught by a student*.

Because most respondents to the questionnaire stated that they wanted one-to-one training, the group set up matched pairs. The matched pairs of trainer and student made their own arrangements about when the training sessions would take place and how long they would last. The pairs also decided between themselves when to end the training.

Before the training began, two members of the computer group developed and printed an easy-to-read set of directions for basic training on Macintosh computers. This printed set of directions was to be part of the file the group decided to keep on each of the trainees. The file was to record progress and problems either the trainer or the trainee encountered. The trainer was responsible for keeping this record. The actual training began on April 23 and continued with some pairs until the Centre closed for the summer on June 11.

Results

The Action Research

On June 4, Wanda asked the following question of everyone who had provided or had taken training in the computer project: "Since the Computer Project started in January, do you feel you use the computers at The Learning Centre more?" Results on this closing survey were as follows:

YES	16 students	53.3%
NO	13 students	43.3%
UNDECIDED	1 student	3.3%

Another measure of the success of the project involved the observations group members made of the growing use of the computers. Some comments group members made on the basis of their observations follow:

> *I think they do [feel comfortable] because now since we started I seen quite a few new students are on the computer.* (Wanda)

> *I've seen people get so excited, they are like, I'm going to be on the computer today. And I'm, like, that's good, that's what you wanted, right?* (Madeline)

> *I mean everybody wants to try it.* (Leona)

> *A lot of people got very interested in the computers and lately I've been noticing that quite a bit.* (Wanda)

The Group Process Research

The results of the research on how the group worked to solve a problem are presented under two headings related to two categories: how this collection of individuals became an effective group, and what the group learned that could be useful outside The Learning Centre.

How this collection of individuals became an effective group

While searching the literature on group behaviour, I was struck by the lack of information about group development in an educational setting. There was much written on psychological or emotional aspects of groups, but I found only one article that outlined the stages an educational group might go through. Armstrong and Yarbrough (1996) call this process of becoming a group "acquiring an internal group environment" (p. 34). They state that the process has two components: interdependence and group development. I will utilize the stages of group development outlined by Armstrong and Yarbrough and provide examples showing how the Computer Group moved through them to become a productive group.

1. Shyness. At the beginning of this stage, little learning is accomplished because the members are busy finding their place. Members are reserved and often defer to others, particularly people they do not know. As mentioned above, most of the members of this group were well known to each other, with the exception of Grace. Some members did defer to Grace initially because she was new; others deferred to me because I had power as the group facilitator. Early in the process, when one student made a suggestion to change the name of the group, no decision was made because each member waited for others to agree with the suggestion and no one assumed a leadership role.

2. Focus. This is when the group plans its work. This group's focus was identified very early as members decided they wanted to start a computer training program at The Learning Centre. The difficult part of focusing learning involved identifying the steps this group needed to go through to plan the training program. The assignment of jobs, the development of instruments to collect information and the analysis of responses to these took up a great deal of time during group meetings.

3. Conflict. Conflict is inevitable in the development of any group, and this group was no exception. Individuals in the group were trying to find their place and were frustrated by some decisions and delays during the planning process. *I want to get underway!* expressed the frustration of some members at having to make changes to the questionnaire before it could be used to collect information. Some members also became anxious about the deadlines established by the group. When one member expressed this frustration more vocally than others, the group made an effort to calm her without giving in to the demands made during the outbursts. No one used these outbursts as an opportunity to "get at" anyone else. *We just talked to her and it was OK . . . instead of ignoring her or not talking to her.* (Leona)

4. Solidification. This is when members get to know each others' strengths and weaknesses and they begin to develop interdependence. Here the learning of the Computer Group was easier because members understood the group process and we understood the group's routine. We also began to acknowledge the differences among ourselves and value the various contributions individuals could make to the group task.

> *We learned how to cooperate . . . and [do] planning.* (Ed)

> *We got to see what people are really like and what way they present themselves.* (Ed)

Campbell (1996) states that the acknowledgment of differences contributes toward the development of a sense of community within a student group. "The naming and acknowledgment of differences seems to unite the group" (p. 137). The more time we spent together the more we saw strengths in others.

5. Performance. This is when group learning is greatest because members are aware of the position each member plays, and they are comfortable with the strengths of various members. Our group entered the performance stage when members started the computer training and saw that it was having an impact on the lives of others in the Centre.

> *I feel real good about being a trainer, I guess because you are helping someone else. . . . It makes you feel good.* (Leona)

> *I felt good about it. I thought I had ideas and I used someone else's ideas and stuff. We worked together excellent.* (Wanda)

Armstrong and Yarbrough say that the facilitator of the group should initially be responsible for understanding the group's internal environment, but at different times other members need to take on that responsibility. Madeline and another member, at various times, took on the role of conflict mediator. Wanda and Ed sometimes took on the role of joker to relieve tension. Some members took little responsibility for group internal environment. Their choice to remain silent could have come from past experience in group work where they were not heard or from an inability to follow the discussion (Campbell, 1996).

I should point out these stages are not intended to be separate and distinct. Members may go through these stages as described, they may go through the stages more quickly or they may skip stages. Individual personality plays a role in how each member moves through these group development components. For example, Madeline and Leona spent little time at the politeness stage and more at the focus and performance stages, while Joyce and Robert continued at the politeness stage through most of the group meetings. Wanda changed over time. She saw her own strength early and contributed significantly during the performance stage.

What the group learned that could be useful outside of The Learning Centre

Imel (1996) refers to the need to establish a balance between process and content for group learning to be effective. The process, what members learned about themselves and how a group works, were discussed above and are also included in this section. In addition this section describes skills group members gained and how group members felt they had affected the community of The Learning Centre.

When asked directly "What have you learned from the group?" members talked about new social skills and technical skills interchangeably. Some of the comments about the social skills the group members acquired follow. Some of these comments focused on what a group can accomplish:

Basically I learned most that with a group we can get things done a lot. (Leona)

As a group we discussed problems. (Wanda)

We need people with different skills. (Madeline)

I thought I had ideas and I used someone else's ideas. (Ed)

I learned how different people think and how they learn. (Joyce)

And you get to know other people that you don't hang around with that much is a good thing too. (Wanda)

Students also talked about the social skills they had acquired on how to work in a group:

You cooperate with people and you compromise . . . when you are working in a group. (Leona)

We learned to respect each other. (Madeline)

Also speaking up when it's my turn and not interrupting others. (Leona)

As individuals developed social skills, some noted related changes in how they viewed themselves. For example, Joyce commented, *I have a lot of self confidence now.*

The most tangible technical skills developed that could be used outside The Learning Centre were the computer skills. Each member, including Betty who initially thought she would learn nothing from the group, enhanced his or her skills.

> *I know more about the computer than when I started. I know about the e-mail and the Internet.* (Betty)

Closely related were changes in how members felt about computers. One member's comment on the change in her attitude toward the computers was echoed by others:

> *At least you are not scared of the computers, you can just sort of fool around with it.* (Leona)

The research the group did to identify the scope of a problem and design a solution was also seen as involving useful skills to be used outside the Centre. Madeline found the questionnaire a helpful tool.

> *The questionnaire . . . I've taken that outside of here and I've used it myself to get some information from people in the Co-op.* (Madeline)

Ed said he learned *how to present different ideas to different programs* and *how to organize something and have those meetings.* He also commented, *I know how to do those pamphlets and videos.*

How did the group work to solve a problem that individuals would not or could not solve themselves? The group provided a safe place where an individual could freely present his or her ideas and receive immediate feedback from his or her peers. The group was the source of ideas and emotional support individuals could use as they wished and needed.

Members' reaction to my interpretation of group development

I presented a draft copy of my interpretation of the group's development, with names attached to various comments, to all members of the Computer Group who were still at The Learning Centre. Betty and Madeline were able to read the document alone and both told me the comments and evaluation were fair. Madeline said the chapter was "real good," although she did find spelling mistakes.

Wanda, Ed, Joyce and I read the document together orally. We stopped many times for clarification of some of the quotes from the literature I had chosen to include. They seemed pleased to be identified and agreed I had attributed comments correctly.

Implication for My Practice

As facilitator of a learning circle at The Learning Centre, I have tried to follow a participatory approach in my practice. I feel the members of our learning circle are involved with the content, or outcome, of their group learning. However, from the results of this research, I recognize the students could be more involved with the process. The process of group development may depend on the type of environment or setting in which a group is working. Part of learning about process would be a better understanding of that environment. "The value in analysing this relationship (between the learning group and its environment) is that it provides insight into group learning as a process as well as an outcome" (Armstrong and Yarbrough, 1996, p. 37).

Participatory approaches in adult education encourage group activities because they give more control and responsibility to the learner (Hayes and Walter, 1995). In my practice I will be looking at group learning in a much broader way, with group process skills being discussed prior to beginning the group learning activity. Part of group process involves conflict, and resolution of conflicts could be part of group process training. In Imel's (1996) opinion, conflict is primarily generated from different personalities and life experiences among members. Once members of a group are aware that these conflicts will arise as a normal part of the group process, they can take steps to deal with them. In my practice I hope to be more aware that social interaction is educational in and of itself.

Reflections on the Research

My purpose for this research was to understand why group work is good for adult learners. I found that most members of the group learned many things about themselves. They learned how to use the group to identify a problem, solve that problem and implement action that affects their immediate environment. However, further research is needed on learning groups in an adult basic education context, with equal emphasis placed on the process and content of the learning.

Armstrong and Yarbrough (1996) agree: "Clearly, adult educators wishing to facilitate group learning need additional information" (p. 34).

Most of the literature I have read on group function deals with group behaviour and development. The next step of applying that knowledge to an educational or learning context is needed. Research on how adults work in learning groups in different subject areas would be helpful. For example, are learning groups in math different from learning groups in reading and writing?

Reflections on the Research Process

The action research completed by the Computer Group at The Learning Centre was valuable work. The group decided to share their learning experience with other adult learners by writing a handbook for other groups or individuals to use to teach themselves how to do a research project about computers. This handbook is the concrete evidence of a year's work. In it the group outlined the struggle they went through to plan and implement meaningful change in their environment at The Learning Centre (Colgan and Pheasey, 2000).

The research skills (planning, interviewing, data analysis, and reflection), computer skills and group process skills that members learned have given most members of the group a better understanding of themselves and their environment and have enhanced their self-esteem. Most of the group members liked doing the research, asking the questions and thinking about what the responses meant.

> *For a change I was the one asking the questions and writing the answers down. It was a switch.* (Leona)

Although group members found it difficult at times to attend meetings and complete tasks, they made an extra effort because the benefit would be coming to the group, not only to themselves as individuals.

The group process component of the research was largely a pleasure. I enjoyed attending the meetings because there was so much enthusiasm among the group members. I found taking field notes, interviewing, transcribing and reflecting on those transcripts to be interesting. I learned a great deal about my practice, not only in relation to my work with the Computer Group but my total involvement at the Centre. My major source of anxiety revolved around data analysis and interpretation. In an attempt to establish trustworthiness for my results, I used many different sources of information, including observations, field notes, interviews, documents and videotapes. I used the informants' own words and developed categories from those words. I also presented a first draft of my results to members of the Computer Group for their feedback on my interpretations. A major challenge was going beyond a "descriptive presentation of the categories" to a "deeper level of interpretation" (Malicky, On-line research unit # 6).

I needed the support of the members of the Computer Group and others to complete this research. The cooperation from other staff and students at The Learning Centre was remarkable.

References

Armstrong, J. L., & Yarbrough, S. L. (1996). Group learning: The role of environment. *New Directions for Adult and Continuing Education, 71,* 33–39.

Auerbach, E. R. (1992). *Making meaning making change. Participatory curriculum development for adult ESL literacy.* McHenry, IL: Delta Systems, Inc.

Campbell, P. (1996). Participatory literacy practices: Exploring social identity and relations. *Adult Basic Education, 6*(1), 127–141.

Colgan, W., & Pheasey, A. (Eds.). (2000). *Students training students: An action research project to help people use computers.* Edmonton, AB: Voices Rising/Learning at the Centre Press.

Hayes, E., & Walter, P. G. (1995). A comparison of small group learning approaches in adult literacy education. *Adult Basic Education, 5*(3), 133–151.

Imel, S. (1996). Summing up: Themes and issues related to learning in groups. *New Directions for Adult and Continuing Education, 71,* 91–96.

Jurmo, P. (1989) The case for participatory literacy education. *New Directions for Continuing Education, 42,* 17-34.

Quigley B. A., & Kuhne, G. W. (1997). Creating practical knowledge through action research: Posing problems, solving problems, and improving daily practice. *New Directions for Adult and Continuing Education, 73,* 3–87.

Appendix A
Group Process Interview Questions

Questions from the First Interview

1. Why did you express an interest in the computer project?

2. Are you interested or do you have any ideas about how the computers should be used?

3. Do you feel comfortable using the computers?

4. Have you felt comfortable learning new things about the computers?

5. Have you had anybody try to teach you how and how did that feel?

6. Do you feel our computer group can help solve this problem?

Questions from the Second Interview

1. How do you feel everything is going with the computer group?

2. What do you think about what happened on Monday? [At the meeting on the previous Monday there was a particularly long and loud dispute with one member, regarding a decision the group had made in her absence.]

3. Do you feel you are listened to?

Appendix B

Questionnaire

NAME_____

1a. Tell me why you don't use the computer.

1b. What do you use the computers for?

2a. Please tell me how much you know about_____.

2b. What would you like to learn on the computers? (✓)

	NOTHING	A LITTLE	ALOT	LIKE TO LEARN
turning it on				
putting disks in and out				
opening a program				
saving work on disk				
Macintosh				
Internet				
e-mail				
World Wide Web				
Print Shop Deluxe				
cards				
posters				
Writing				
word processing				
spell check				
Color It!				
PhotoShop				
Art				
(MS DOS/Windows) MS Word				
word processing				
spell check				

	NOTHING	A LITTLE	ALOT	LIKE TO LEARN
Fractions Made Easy				
Database				
Art				
Games Solitaire				
Typing help				

3. What else do you want to learn how to do on the computer?

4. How do you want to learn the computer?

_____with a tutor (one-on-one)

_____in a group (3 or 4 people)

_____in a class (everybody together)

_____by watching someone do it and then trying it out yourself

INTERVIEWER_____

Appendix C

Findings from the Questionnaire

1a.   Why don't you use the computer?

13	–	don't know how
5	–	need help
6	–	no time or rather stay in class
2	–	never used or don't use much
2	–	have own computer at home
3	–	other (want Macintosh computers back; sometimes do, sometimes don't; sometimes don't have any stories)

1b.   What do you use the computers for?

21	–	writing or writing stories
8	–	nothing
3	–	games
3	–	letters

1 each for e-mail, cards, poems, typing help

3.   What else do you want to learn?

10	–	named something on the list
10	–	everything on the list
4	–	spelling
4	–	math
2	–	basic things
2	–	other (alphabet, learning English)

4.   How do you want to learn the computer?

25	–	with a tutor (one-on-one)
9	–	in a group
3	–	in a class
7	–	by watching somebody do it and then trying it out yourself

Chapter 5

Listening to Drum Beats Around a Northern Campus: Practitioner Based Research in a First Nations Community

Audrey Fofonoff

Audrey Fofonoff

Listening to Drum Beats Around a Northern Campus: Practitioner Based Research in a First Nations Community

Our Program and My Role in It

I live and work in a primarily First Nations and Metis community north of Edmonton, Alberta. From my perspective the community is fascinating in the contrast of the people's reliance on hunting and some traditional ways and their participation in forestry and an oil and gas-based economy. The juxtapostion of sometimes-opposing forms of livelihood means that the community is in the process of considerable change. Less than ten years ago, before the highway from the nearest town was paved, people here were isolated from urban centres. Today, the people who live here travel as needed to larger towns with more services less than two hours away, and also to Edmonton, which is about four hours away.

Our campus generally has a population of between 100 and 150 adult students in academic upgrading programs. In March 1997 I accepted a teaching contract to pilot a class of eleven Basic Education Level (BEL) 1 students. Prior to that time students who came to the college with minimal reading and writing skills were placed with BEL 2 students. I was given the responsibility of developing a Real Life Reading curriculum for the adults in BEL 1. This responsibility has since extended to modifying the curricula and expanding resources in the BEL 2 Real Life Reading and Communications courses. In developing the Real Life Reading course I have focused on social studies topics related to the history of northwestern Canada, and health topics related to the concerns of our community.

In the fall of 1997, our campus director encouraged me to investigate whether or not I would like to become involved in the Participatory Approaches in Adult Literacy Education/Research in Practice Project. As a newcomer to our campus and to 1990s literacy developments in Alberta, I welcomed the opportunity to become involved. I saw benefits in familiarizing myself with literacy practices in Alberta and in evaluating my own practices. This project could allow me to be more accountable to my students in ongoing curriculum development, an area in which I had extensive experience and interest.

The project described in this paper can be categorized as practitioner-initiated descriptive research. My research goal was to determine if a series of theme-related activities incorporating listening, observing, writing, reading and questioning/discussion skills would enhance students' knowledge about the encompassing theme of Cree culture and lifestyle. I worked with ever-changing groups of adult students in Basic Education Level classes at our campus. The activities that I observed for the purposes of the project were as follows: group reading and evaluation of two books introduced to the BEL program, a field trip to a museum, and a writers' workshop. In some of these activities students at levels other than BEL 1 and 2 were also involved.

Vision Underlies Our Practice—We All Have It

As Suzanne Hale (1998) so delightfully and honestly explains, it is literacy teachers' convictions that compel us to continue when the realities of research-in-action entangle us. To persevere throughout the research in practice project reported in this book, when its dimensions grew beyond our original expectations, we had to feel strong in the beliefs that propel us in our daily practice.

Early in the project (March 1998), while I immersed myself in readings, I reflected upon Osborne's *Teaching for democratic citizenship* and began thinking about political perspective. Now and in the past I have hoped that careful teaching can contribute to social change within our political system. I also place importance on understanding "the relationships among ideology, power, culture and curriculum" (Osborne, 1991, p. 50). From my experience, many textbooks and programs ignore or misrepresent the history of women, Native people, non-famous people and people from minority groups. I was raised in a minority culture that values passive, but stubborn, resistance to war and injustice, so I see the world from that perspective. I think it is this view that drives me to continually search for learning materials that represent other minorities and groups of people whose points of view are under-articulated. This approach to teaching was encouraged in my encounter with Frontier College in 1974, and it is one I have developed since the early 1980s when I began work as a literacy instructor.

I also see my role as providing access to information that students request and nurturing critical thinking skills. This is consistent with what Hayes and Walter (1995) describe in relation to collaborative literacy approaches:

> The teacher still has primary responsibility for designing the learning activities, presumably drawing on the self-identified needs and backgrounds of learners. (p.138)

I do not see my role as coinciding with what I understand from some of the popular education literature. I don't think it is realistic to create activist attitudes in the students I work with. Some of them may already be activists in their lives. I can help them improve some of their communication skills, but I think the initiative to create change was theirs to begin with and remains theirs.

From life experiences, I have come to believe that sobriety is a key element in achieving positive changes in communities. Staying away from drugs and alcohol is essential to the optimum health and strong self-esteem that I see as necessary elements in positive change. An underlying assumption in my practice is that women's health during pregnancy has a lasting effect on the generations that follow. Ability to learn easily in various ways is forever linked to the prenatal environment of each person. I feel that I should provide my students with information about the consequences of drinking alcohol during pregnancy, because Fetal Alcohol Syndrome is a pervasive concern in many cultures and societies.

During my search for culturally-relevant ways to teach at my present location, I learned enough about Cree culture to feel stronger in my resolve to practice and speak about a lifestyle without alcohol. Denys Auger of the Bigstone Cree Nation is a pipe carrier and keeper of the land. According to him (February 2000, personal communication),

> It has never been the practice of Native people who are strong believers of spirituality to mix the use of alcohol with the practice of their beliefs. In fact, in the 1950s some people in the North stopped their ceremonies out of respect for their spiritual lodges because alcohol's destructive aspects began to be seen by them. One of the unwritten laws of respect for traditional beliefs was that a kind heart, clear mind and clean spirit would be destroyed by alcohol. Use of alcohol is a complete digression from the values that are the basis of traditional Native culture. It is only since the late 1980s that Native spiritual ceremonies have begun to be practiced again. This pause in traditional practices had in fact been predicted by the elders. Their teachings were that alcohol would destroy

the Native people. So the abstention from alcohol is closely linked to the rejuvenation of spiritual and cultural knowledge in this area.

Another underlying assumption that guides my practice is the belief that I should include analyses of consumerism and the effects of advertising in my curriculum choices. Our lives are heavily influenced by the current political drive toward a global market economy powered by uncritical consumerism. My view is that educational curricula should help students be aware of this. I feel hopeful that within each culture there are ways to work against this global trend to excess consumerism. Unless we resist it with knowledge and action, it tends to leave us feeling powerless to attain sustainable livelihoods that will not cause irreparable damage to our natural environment.

My growing understanding of the Cree people's perspective on the environment strengthens my views on this issue. Recently, Denys Auger told me that keeping a healthy land base is essential in the practice of traditional culture for Native people because it revolves around the four elements of land, air, water and fire. He says,

> In learning about Cree culture you will never put it in words to please everyone. Cree culture is one of the richest cultures. You learn about the mind, body and spirit. The four elements all have strong spirits. It is endless to learn, and you are thankful at the end.

For me the link between my belief system and what I have learned about the theme of Cree culture during the past two years has been a satisfying dimension of my work on this project.

My Previous Experience in Literacy Curriculum Development

My work life has taken me to places far from my original home and cultural group. As a newcomer to each community, I feel excited about bringing to the people ideas, stories, and experiences from adults I have previously worked with. I also realize the need to open my eyes and heart to the local ways. I have become comfortable with bringing with me a few materials developed by students and teachers in the places I've previously been, and immediately encouraging the development of indigenous ones. I know, too, that the process of creation of local materials takes longer than a year. When I begin in a new program, I try to provide an environment for adult students to share their views on life and issues with me and with others in the groups of six to 15 students that I work with during any one class period.

Before beginning work at this campus, I worked in adult literacy in St. John's, Newfoundland between 1981 and 1997, with the exception of two years of literacy work in Calgary in the late 1980s. My primary area of interest has been curriculum development around local themes. While teaching, I have often needed to rewrite existing fictional and non-fictional literature to make it more accessible to adults with basic literacy skills. With my co-workers I also revised some government pamphlets about real life issues into plain English. We did the same with numerous items from newspapers. While working at Cabot College of Applied Arts, Technology and Continuing Education in St. John's, I co-edited several volumes of the *Write Now* (1995) series of students' writings. I also co-authored *Starting Points* (1995), resource materials in social studies, geography and science that were written to meet the needs of Adult Basic Education (ABE) Level 1 students at that college.

The drive to create student-centred materials for use in literacy arose from my encounters with various American literacy workbooks as early as 1981. I was appalled with the prevalence of such literacy materials, which were without relevance for my students in Newfoundland. Since then I have developed curricula around what I determined were my students' interests and around issues important to me because of the influences and values of my own minority culture. I deeply appreciate the freedom of continuous curriculum development that working in adult literacy has thus far allowed me.

During the university course component of the Participatory Approaches in Adult Literacy Education Project, I became increasingly aware that many of my decisions about ongoing curriculum development are based on observing and sensing students' interests. I also realized that I could do more to encourage students' involvement, consciously, at many stages in the planning of a student-centred curriculum, its creation, and its evaluation. This seemed an area of my practice that I could work on, having made a commitment to participate in the project for a year.

How I Determined the Research Goal

As an instructor in the early stages of building rapport with students in my groups, I determined the research goal without direct student involvement. However, I did rely on my students' responses to 30 questions about activities and topics covered during the fall term, which I discussed with them in January. The series of questions was a way to get some written feedback from them about activities I had attempted. Until then their interests and opinions had not been articulated so I did not actually know what they were thinking. The students' responses revealed that many were interested in finding out more about Cree culture, traditions and lifestyles.

The students' expressed interest coincided with my assumption that one benefits from being saturated with knowledge about one's own culture before relating to a wider world view. Of all that we read during the course portion of this project, I identify most with writings by Elsa Auerbach. Of special interest is her paper "The power of voices and the voices of power" (1997). At our campus I see a place for Auerbach's view that "only when local ways of knowing, literacy practices, languages, and cultural knowledge are included and valued will literacy and education be empowering" (p. 3). The main point that I gained from reading Auerbach's work was that rather than privately assimilate feedback from students, it is useful to bring their ideas back to the group to discuss openly. I sensed my need to learn to feel less vulnerable about this process.

Thus, during the early stages of the project reported in this paper, the students' articulated goal was to learn about Cree culture and lifestyle. My goal was to determine if a series of theme-related activities incorporating listening, observing, writing, reading and questioning/discussion skills would enhance learning about the encompassing theme of Cree culture and lifestyle. My concurrent goal as a teacher was to practise ways in which I could relinquish some of my habitual leadership role in the classroom at appropriate times to allow students' voices to strengthen within our classroom groups and possibly beyond in the community.

Profile of the Adult Students in the Project

At our campus, the second term of the 1997/1998 Academic Year began on February 2. A replacement instructor from another campus of our college worked with my students for the first six weeks of the term while I was on surgery leave. On March 16, I returned full-time to work with the literacy students in Basic Education Levels 1 and 2. At that time I worked with the following groups:

BEL 1 Group. There were three men and four women in this group; two were non-readers. I met with this group every morning. Usually, half our time was spent on reading/discussion activities and half on developing basic math skills. We spent half of Friday morning in the computer lab using Microsoft Word or Typing Tutor. This group worked with other instructors for communications classes and mathematics tutorials during the afternoons.

BEL 2a Group. The three men and nine women in this group worked with two other instructors during the mornings. I worked with them in Real Life Reading for 80-minute blocks four afternoons each week.

BEL 2b Group. The three men and ten women in this group also worked with two other instructors during the mornings. I saw them for Real Life Reading during 80-minute blocks four afternoons each week, separately from the BEL 2a group.

During the early part of the winter/spring term, on any given day, I met with all or some of the 32 students in these groups, depending on their attendance. I had one hour of planning time available to me between 3:30 and 4:30 Monday to Thursday, in addition to all of Friday afternoon.

Of the 32 students, 24 had attended adult basic upgrading since September 1997; eight began in February 1998. This meant that in the initial stages of the project in late March, I had known some of the students for only two weeks. On the other hand, I had known some of the women for one year; that is, since my arrival at this campus.

Almost all students in the BEL 1 and 2 groups are Cree or Metis in their cultural background. Many are Cree-speaking and would consider English to be a second language. Even students in their twenties may have experienced some aspects of a traditional Cree lifestyle. At the time of the project, the students ranged from 17 to over 50 years of age.

Students from the BEL 1 and 2 groups participated in the four project activities outlined below. As well, students from high school courses at our campus participated in the field trip and writers' workshop on *The Cree People*. In reality, there is considerable interaction amongst our various academic levels at this campus, so my choice to include the high school level students seemed appropriate. Up to 100 students at various levels of academic upgrading were in attendance at our campus during that term.

The Project Activities

I observed four theme-related activities for the purpose of the project. It is important to note, however, that the four activities were not implemented because of the project. Rather they came about as I gradually learned what is meaningful to my students. My learning about what interests them continued during and after the project.

The four activities that I systematically observed for the purposes of the project were as follows:

- reading and evaluation of *Roast moose and rosaries* by Fred and Mary Courtoreille with BEL 1 and 2a groups

- reading and evaluation of *The Cree People* by Phyllis Cardinal with the BEL 2b group

- visit to the Gallery of Aboriginal Culture at the Provincial Museum in Edmonton on May 5, 1998

- writers' workshop on May 11 to 15, 1998

Collecting Information

The main way I collected information was through questionnaires. The questionnaires relating to the reading and evaluation of the two books were designed to see if the materials would be useful for basic education classes at our campus and other campuses of our college. While collecting detailed information for that purpose, I also included questions specifically related to learning about culture.

After I developed these questions, I read them aloud and explained them to the students prior to asking them to dictate or write their responses. I have always felt more comfortable with written ways of communicating my ideas rather than speaking about them. Focusing on written responses, therefore, was logical for me. Also, many of the students I work with prefer to express their ideas privately through writing rather than in class discussions. I used questionnaires as follows:

- *Roast moose and rosaries* on June 11, 1998, and January 19, 1999 (*see* Appendix A)
- *The Cree People* on March 16, 1998, and January 19, 1999 (*see* Appendix B)
- The field trip to the Gallery of Aboriginal Culture from May 27 to June 9, 1998 (*see* Appendix C)
- The writers' workshop from May 27 to June 9, 1998 (*see* Appendix D)

In addition to the questionnaires, stories written during the writers' workshop were a source of information. In this report, I have included my analysis of the thematic content of stories read during the Writing Jamboree. I also made project notes between January 2 and May 22, 1998, and personal journal entries in March and December of that year. I incorporated these in my reflections about the research process at the end of this report.

Ethical Considerations

Participants in this project formed loosely defined groups with changing boundaries, depending on which of the four main activities they were taking part in. Change is a reality when many people attend and leave campus according to the demands from their daily lives upon them. This presented a problem for me when I struggled with how to obtain informed consent from my students for involvement in the research. I did not have one highly-committed small group of project participants with whom I could frequently discuss and write about project findings. What conversations about classroom interactions could I take out of the context of the classes? Moreover, I sensed that the very process of having students sign consent forms for release of information might cause a barrier between me and the people with whom I was just beginning to form trust bonds. I addressed the informed consent issue by including a request for using the students' ideas for this report with each questionnaire I gave them.

Summaries of students' responses to questionnaires have been included in this report because I felt assured that students from all the academic upgrading levels at our campus, whether they were members of my groups or not, could agree knowingly to sharing their views by signing the consent on the questionnaire.

Analysing Information

The collation of the students' responses seemed to take forever. At one point, I included in my report everything that I had collated from the questionnaires. It all seemed useful to me in my practice. I recognized though, with Mary Norton's guidance, that I needed to make decisions about which data related to my research question.

From an examination of students' responses on the questionnaires and their written stories, I identified the following categories: content related to Cree culture that students were learning; recognition of their own and others' knowledge about culture; and the value they placed on learning about culture. Students also spoke about self-esteem and gaining confidence to write, read, and share their own knowledge through stories.

What I Found Through the Four Activities

Readings of *Roast Moose and Rosaries* with BEL 1 and 2a Groups

The activity

My sister Marcie Fofonoff, who lives in Moberly Lake, British Columbia, gave me the book *Roast moose and rosaries* by Fred and Mary Courtoreille as a Christmas gift. Although several stories in the book are written in Fred and Mary's dialect of English, I thought the book would be readable at a literacy student's level. The content of the stories touched upon at least two experiences shared by many people in northern Alberta: the residential school and traditional bush life. Students were encouraged, but not forced, to read segments of the stories aloud in groups no larger than 15 people. A few people opted out of class readings and discussions because the stories brought back painful memories.

During the spring of 1998, BEL 1, 2a and 2b students read segments of the book aloud in class. However, the end-of-term sample of questionnaires requesting students' evaluations of the book was very small. By June, when I prepared the questions, only three students, all of whom were in BEL 2a, returned the questionnaires to me. At that point, we had read approximately half of the book. The three students agreed to have their comments included in my research.

A second set of questionnaires was gathered from students in January 1999. This sample was larger, as it included evaluations by nine BEL 2a students and two BEL 1 students who had read the entire book during the fall term. Eight people consented to having their responses included in my research.

What I found

People indicated that the book was readable and that they liked its appearance. Four students liked the idea of having the authors' black and white photos on the cover; one person said that the looks of the book brought back memories of how she was brought up. They also mentioned that they liked the humour in the book.

Learning about culture. Students who responded to the questionnaire saw similarities between their lives and those of Mary and Fred in northern British Columbia. One student said her parents had been to a residential school. Ten felt that they learned about the Cree people. They saw similarities between the BC Indians and Indians here [their terms]; they learned about survival off the land in the past, life in the bush and their Cree language; and they learned about the authors' suffering and their strength and will to go on.

Recognizing own experience and cultural knowledge. In response to the question, "Is the book about issues that are real-life issues in your community?" students answered as follows:

- *Some people in this area are still living like they did in the olden days and everyone will be living that way in the near future.*
- *Women continue to be beaten and fighting continues.*
- *Trapping and herbal medicine are still practised here.*
- *Ceremonial dances are held.*
- *Moosehide is used for clothing.*
- *People go to Lac Ste. Anne every year to pray.*

The book reminded one student of her parents' and grandparents' talk about this region. Another student said she would like to live like her grandparents lived. Still another saw similarities in these stories and the ones she had written about her childhood before she had read *Roast moose and rosaries.*

Valuing this learning. Students indicated that they valued the book by sharing it with others and saying it would be worth sharing with people of all ages in the community.

Using this resource

From the students' evaluations of *Roast moose and rosaries*, I concluded that the book is an appropriate choice for group readings and discussion for students in BEL 1 and 2. I feel confident that it is a suitable print resource for learning about Cree culture through reading stories and questioning/discussion about them. It appears that, because the stories were written by people like themselves, my students increasingly placed value on their own stories and photographs.

Reading of *The Cree People* with BEL 2b Groups

The activity

Our library assistant brought a copy of *The Cree People* by Phyllis Cardinal to our staff room. Its content and photographs appealed to me so I asked several students in my classes what they thought of it. Some people recognized relatives or acquaintances, and I heard comments of interest from the people who saw it. I ordered it for the winter term, hoping that it would provide an understanding of essential social studies terms from the perspective of the predominant cultural group in this area, the Cree.

Leslie Sargunaraj, the instructor who replaced me while I was on a surgery leave, used *The Cree People* with BEL 2b students. He followed the pattern of in-class reading aloud by students accompanied by discussion and instructor explanations. Leslie prepared comments about his observations of the students' attitude toward the book. His comments are included in Appendix E. Five students from Leslie's group shared their views of *The Cree People* with me in March 1998.

In January 1999, I gathered a second sample of evaluations by a 2b group I worked with during the fall term. This evaluation was based on the first four chapters of the book, whereas the first sample was based on the entire book. Four students completed the evaluation. Of these four, three agreed to share their views for the purposes of the project.

What I found

Most students said the reading level was comfortable although one said that some words were difficult. They were pleased with the appearance of the book, including the cover and photographs. One person would have preferred a smaller-size book because the size made it look like a children's book. Five people said that the book was very interesting.

Recognizing own experience and cultural knowledge. One student liked the appearance of the book because it shows many Indian people. Some said they recognized people they knew. One person said, "It was exciting to read about something you've seen happening in your own life."

Learning about culture. Comments such as the following suggest that students learned about culture, history and government:

- *It showed how Cree culture was years ago and how it is today.*
- *I learned a lot about my culture: Indian Act, residential schools.*
- *It helped me to understand governments' past efforts to help Cree people, their mistakes, what they are doing today to try to improve things.*
- *It gave information about treaty names and explained self-government; now I know what another Band wants.*

Another student mentioned learning about cultural differences amongst people and changes that took place in Cree culture, as well as learning about legends and the hunting/gathering lifestyle.

Valuing this learning. As with *Roast moose and rosaries*, some students shared *The Cree People* with family members and neighbours, and they said that other people in the community were interested in the book. Someone mentioned that young Cree people should read this book to help keep their Native identity and language, and to learn about their culture. One person said that there was more for Cree people to learn than was in the book, such as knowledge of hunting and of healing through Indian medicine.

Using this resource

From my observations during this project, *The Cree People* appears to be at a reading level that is too high for BEL 1 and 2a, but suitable in guided group readings for BEL 2b. At the 2b level, *The Cree People* did enhance learning about the theme of Cree culture and lifestyle through group readings and discussion. I frequently suggest journal writing on this theme following our current readings of portions of chapters. To find out more about the topics mentioned in this book, I invite local presenters and I show videos from the *My partners—My people* series, and the *Daughters of the country* series. Several students have been active in suggesting which local presenters I should invite.

Through using the book with my classes, I have discovered that the very word "culture" can create uncomfortable feelings in a community where certain religions promote a mistrust of Native spirituality and traditional ceremonies. For this reason, the topics in *The Cree People* must be introduced with awareness of these differences in the community.

I use questions and activities in the teacher's manual selectively because they were prepared for junior high students rather than adults. Many of the review and test pages in the manual do help to reinforce the vocabulary that the author introduces. Repetition of these key words is useful in helping my students understand the English language used by the author to describe Cree culture, which was largely oral, visual and practical, rather than written.

Visit to the Gallery of Aboriginal Culture

The activity

The decision to visit the Gallery of Aboriginal Culture at the Provincial Museum on May 5, 1998, in Edmonton was consistent with ongoing efforts at our campus to make our curriculum culturally relevant and participatory for students in the BEL program. I also saw the field trip as an opportunity to observe the effects of a visual and auditory activity on increasing our students' cultural awareness. I hoped that the visit to the gallery would act as a catalyst for written expression of students' ideas about their culture. The field trip and the writers' workshop were scheduled within the same month to allow maximum complementary activities to develop. I also hoped that the background reading we had done during the fall and winter in the two books that the students read for this project would be helpful in clarifying the topic of Cree culture, and that this knowledge would enhance their experience at the museum.

In the early stages of planning the field trip, I felt the museum visit would appeal to our student population across academic levels. Although students in BEL classes were given the first opportunity to sign up, the trip was open to interested high school students at our campus well in advance of our departure to Edmonton. During the field trip, the adult high school students who went had the opportunity to practise their research skills as a component of high school level English.

Of the 38 people who signed up, 13 students from across all academic levels at our campus actually went on the trip. Seven were from classes that I worked with. I distributed the questionnaires to students who went on the trip in late May and June 1998. Of the eight participants who returned their written responses about the trip to me, six agreed to have their comments included in this report. I also asked people in my BEL classes who went on the trip to share their impressions with others who had not. Their comments about what they learned provided additional information to that on the questionnaires.

Students toured the exhibits in groups of two without a museum guide. They observed the artifacts and murals, read some of the captions, and listened to the audio tapes on their own. In these ways the tour was consistent with my research goal.

What I found

I was unable to determine whether or not the prior readings we had done helped the seven BEL students who went on the trip to understand the exhibits. None of the writings read during the writers' workshop, nor those in the students' collection of stories, were about the field trip or the exhibits. Hence, there were no evident connections between the trip and the other three activities, but there were many shared themes between the museum exhibits and *The Cree People*.

On the questionnaire, I asked why people went to the Gallery of Aboriginal Culture. While some went out of curiosity or to get away from home for a while, one woman said she wanted to know more about her cultural heritage. She said that it helped her to find where she was from and who she is.

Learning about culture. Most of the students who went to the museum indicated that they learned positive aspects of their culture during the tour. They made comments such as the following:

- *It was interesting to see tools and weapons that people used to survive.*
- *I now understand the way of life of my ancestors.*
- *We saw lots of beadwork—it must have been a lot of work.*

When discussing highlights of the visit, students mentioned learning about traditional medicines and the challenges of surviving off the land.

Recognizing own experience and cultural knowledge. One man mentioned that despite having lost interest in his culture while growing up in a convent, he had recognized objects his grandfather had told him stories about, such as copper pails, axes, powder shotguns and tomahawks.

Valuing this learning. One woman expressed a desire to learn more about ceremonies and about George Wabasca, a major in World War I, whom she read about at the gallery. Another student suggested going on a trip to someone's bush camp near campus. After the trip to the gallery one person said, *We have a lot to be proud of as Native people.*

Writers' Workshop

The activity

The idea of having a week-long workshop to elicit storytelling from the students on our campus germinated in October 1997 during an informal conversation between me and friends of mine through my previous literacy work, Larry Loyie and Constance Brissenden. Larry and Constance form the Living Traditions Writers Group in Vancouver, British Columbia. A workshop with them seemed like an excellent opportunity for students to share oral stories and write with two experienced writers who are very familiar with and encourage a First Nations perspective. Moreover, as a young boy, Larry had experienced a traditional Cree life in this northern region.

From my perspective in the participatory approaches project, I thought such a workshop could involve students at our campus in the creation and evaluation of ongoing curriculum development in the literacy program at our college. As a beginning, a collection of students' writings could come out of such an event. I realized that the workshop would provide an avenue for learning primarily through listening, discussion and oral presentation, with less of an emphasis on reading. Students would have an opportunity to be expressive and participatory during the workshop, and also they could evaluate it afterwards.

I thought that the two reading sources, *Roast moose and rosaries* and *The Cree People*, which had been used in my classes throughout that academic year, could serve as reminders to the students of what they already knew about their own culture. I hoped those readings would encourage research into their own family and community backgrounds. I also hoped that the field trip to the Gallery of Aboriginal Culture, which had taken place only a week before the workshop, would be a catalyst to writing.

From previous experience, I knew the value of having a published collection of local students' writings. This idea is not a novel one; I find that invariably people are interested in seeing stories written by themselves and by people they know in published form. I had initiated the four activities that I observed for the participatory approaches project with the expectation that they would complement each other and culminate in a collection of student writings from our campus.

Our local Community Education Committee (CEC) generously funded Larry and Constance as guest instructors for a week at our campus. The CEC continued their support by pledging funds toward the publishing of the students' collection of writings, which was completed by June 1998 (*Âcimowina: Storytelling*, 2000).

More than thirty students at various levels of reading and writing ability took part in the week-long writers' workshop. Some participated in several sessions; others also took time to meet with Constance and Larry on their own to talk about pieces they had written. In addition to giving presentations of Larry's own work and mini-lectures about writing from the heart, the writers offered the following sessions:

- Script writing based on videos
- Photo stories
- Narration with dialogue
- Writing down oral histories and community traditions
- Composing a group poem

On May 15 we held a Writing Jamboree on our campus. During the week students were invited either to read their own stories aloud at the Jamboree, or to allow someone else, such as an instructor, to read their story. The atmosphere at this event was wonderful. Listeners were alert and respectful as the heart-warming stories were read.

In late May and June of 1998, I distributed a questionnaire about the workshop to the students of all academic upgrading levels at our campus. Twenty-four of the students who had taken part in the workshop answered the questionnaire; 18 agreed to let me use their comments. The written text of the stories that were read during the Jamboree were another source for my research. I compiled a list of themes in the students' stories read during the Jamboree. I felt comfortable analysing these stories because all students consented to having their stories published; hence, these stories were public documents.

What I found

Through the writers' workshop and the Writing Jamboree many students learned about Cree culture and lifestyle by listening, writing and reading. In addition to the themes described below, the week-long event appeared to increase students' self-esteem. From observation of people's interactions and attention to comments between readings by instructors and students during the Writing Jamboree, it was evident that students who submitted their readings for public hearing, (particularly those who read their own stories aloud) showed courage to do so. They stretched their boundaries of personal privacy and they challenged their fear of possible ridicule by listeners.

Recognizing own experience and cultural knowledge. A number of students suggested that they enhanced their understanding or appreciation of their culture. They mentioned that they learned about the local people's culture, about traditional ways and people of the past. One person realized she had many worthwhile stories to write.

Valuing this learning. On the questionnaires many students commented that they gained skills and confidence to write and read in front of a group. For example, one student mentioned learning to trust the writers and the other students, and to respect himself for what he did. Another learned that anyone could write and she decided she could write more about a community she had lived in. Others said they learned to write stories, either their own, or a relative's.

Students' suggestions for future workshops. From a list I had compiled for the questionnaire, I asked students to indicate choices for future workshops. Writing stories was the most popular choice. Smoking fish or meat, traditional medicines and basket making were in the middle range of choices. Students' own suggestions included trips away from town to pursue traditional land-based activities.

From my analysis of the stories read during the Writing Jamboree, I identified a number of themes that support the comments students made on the questionnaires about the writing workshop. Interactions amongst people in extended families were often mentioned. These interactions included a willingness to help others in need, courage in isolated areas, a deep appreciation of learning skills from their parents, and excitement from being on the land. Some examples of references related to the theme of learning traditional land-based skills were as follows: hunting for muskrats, setting nets for fish, eating duck soup, skinning moose, drinking moose blood, and setting snares. References were also made to providing support or helping to deliver babies in situations distant from hospital. Some of the stories were appreciative of knowledge shared by grandparents.

Another recurring theme in written stories was a spiritual connection with loved ones who had passed on. One person described a strong premonition surrounding the tragic death of a family member. Others wrote about a belief in spirit animals and a connection with one's spirit self, as in the description of a powwow. Some stories dealt with tragic deaths and other sad events, such as living in foster homes. In several stories warm humour about situations or incidents was evident. One student wrote about the importance of expressing her ideas through poetry to the extent of saying that writing was a way of wanting to live, a struggle against suicidal thoughts.

Overall, the students' collection of stories indicated interest in learning about Cree culture and lifestyle. Perhaps the Writing Jamboree was an opportunity to celebrate culture as well as to share knowledge about it. While the other project activities were mainly about reading or absorbing information, during the Writers' Workshop, people generated and shared knowledge.

Applying What I Learned

This report was completed two years after the project began. Both books that the students read and evaluated during the project continue to be primary resources in the BEL 1 and 2 classrooms at our campus. Moreover, they have been added to the resources list for our college, and are now used at other campuses. Another instructor and I have compiled questions for each story in *Roast moose and rosaries*.

At our campus we have continued to add additional resources on the theme of northern Cree culture and lifestyle. (*See* resource list at the end of this chapter.) I will continue to add more published resources which expand our knowledge on this theme as I become aware of them. I will also continue to include other non-print ways of learning. During the past two years, several resource people from the band have willingly shared their knowledge of local issues in my literacy classrooms. In this way my knowledge of the local ways has broadened at least as much as that of my students. I hope to continue this cooperative relationship between the community and our campus.

Several students and I took photographs during the 1998 field trip. I had hoped to use these photos as catalysts for photo stories during the writers' workshop less than a week later, but this plan was scrapped because we could not develop them quickly enough. However, the photo story session during the writers' workshop went ahead. Students who had brought 1940s and 1950s photographs from their families' collections earlier that term gave permission for us to use them during the workshop.

Our picture taking did not stop there. Early in the following fall semester, I suggested students take photos of sites and activities in our community that were meaningful to them. I provided my camera and said that I would drive to the locations where they could photograph subjects of their choice. This activity helped me take a non-leadership role. I was particularly pleased with one student's invitation to let us photograph her drying moose meat.

A year after the trip, six students and some instructors from our campus went on a three-day trip to Jasper National Park. We built upon the experience of our previous trip to the Gallery of Aboriginal Culture when organizing the 1999 trip.

Immediately following the writers' workshop, two of the women who had read stories during the Writing Jamboree submitted them to the June issue of their band's newspaper. When I asked them how that felt, both said they felt positive about doing so. During the fall of 1998 I included a description of our workshop in our college newsletter. That prompted a request from the editors for students' stories from our campus. Several of our students were pleased to send in their stories from the jamboree, and two of those were published in the November/December college newsletter. These stories were read aloud in our classes, so the excitement of seeing stories from our campus in published form spread. Another participant in the workshop sent some of her stories and a photograph to the May/June issue of *English Express* the next year.

Challenges and Benefits of Research in Practice

Challenges

The biggest challenge throughout my involvement with the project has been my reluctance to work beyond my full-time work schedule. My full-time work is not extraordinarily stressful, but it does require focus and mental and physical energy. I find, too, that in my forties I will not often "burn midnight oil" and overextend myself for important causes as I did in the previous two decades of my life. A life where I spend time in fitness activities, in leisure, and with my family, in addition to my work schedule, is increasingly important to me. The longer the research in practice project extended, the more these conscious choices began to interfere with my commitment to it. I felt the least torn between my priorities during the participatory approaches phase in May and June 1998, when I was able to work at the college and participate in the project simultaneously, largely within my scheduled seven-hour work day.

During the university course component of the project, which began while I was recovering from surgery, and during the several months of the data analysis and report-writing, I had to repeatedly summon the energy to work beyond a 37 to 40 hour work week. I felt I had to make choices in allocating time for my work life. Repeatedly, I focused on my involvement with my students rather than on collecting and analysing the data for the research phase of the project. For me, the lasting value was in asking the adults with whom I worked for frequent feedback of what we do at the campus, rather than in recording the results of this particular research on paper.

Moreover, I felt hampered by not owning a computer. When I needed one to write this paper, I had to return to my workplace on weekends or evenings. I do not, however, write easily in short segments but instead need blocks of solitude to mull over and organize my ideas on paper.

Although there was project money to pay for a teaching substitute for me, this was not a realistic option because of the difficulty of getting qualified substitutes for short periods of time at our northern campus. Perhaps a two-week non-teaching block of time in the fall of 1998 and another week in the spring of 1999 would have made it possible to analyse the data more thoroughly than I have. This is something to consider for those who begin research in practice projects.

A few specific problems occurred with my data collection. As described in the report, continuity, confidentiality and requesting permission of my students were challenges for me. These could possibly be addressed more easily with a short-term project of several months involving fewer participants.

What I did not realize at the time when I formulated my research goal is that it is useful to have a baseline of recorded observations about an issue or practice at the start of a project. Now I realize that the research question should be precise, manageable in our context and, preferably, worded by the participants.

Some of the questions I developed for the questionnaires could have been worded in a more understandable way for my students. For example, in *The Cree People* questionnaire, the question about whether their outlook had changed as a result of reading the book was too difficult because the word "outlook" was not understood. Another question about whether or not the book was carefully researched was also problematic. Likely, the students had no way of determining this.

Benefits

On the benefits side, I do not regret the opportunity to discuss literacy practices with the other women in the project, and I very much appreciate Mary Norton and Grace Malicky's wisdom and encouragement at each stage. Their timelines were generous and flexible throughout my involvement. During the course segment of the project and during the participatory approaches phase of it in 1998, I enjoyed the energy that frequent exchanges of ideas brings.

With respect to data collection, the use of questionnaires during the project worked for me. Without that structure I would have found it much harder a year later to see what people were saying about learning about culture. Moreover, the questionnaires serve a broader purpose than the project itself. I continue to refer to the students' comments in planning activities at our campus.

The course component of the project reminded me of the benefit of frequently asking for comments about what we do in our classes. I have incorporated this into my practice through regular requests for issue-related journals. I gain useful insights about my students' reactions to activities, speakers, videos, and resources through weekly process journals.

I did not include informal data from my own journal entries and project notes in this published report. My participatory group of students was so changeable over the course of the two years I worked on the project that I did not feel comfortable getting written permission to share anecdotal information. On the other hand, my journal entries helped me to reflect upon the effects of my practice on the students I work with. A second aspect of these notes is that they serve as a record of the challenges I felt during the project and were helpful in writing this segment of the report.

The project provided excellent opportunities for me to meet with other women who have a great commitment to literacy in Alberta. Because several adults from The Learning Centre in Edmonton accompanied Mary Norton to our campus during the project, some of our students had a chance to exchange ideas with adult students from elsewhere.

Presenting our fledgling research in practice projects in November 1998 at the Literacy Conference in Calgary, and at the Research in Practice Seminar in Richmond, helped me to clarify what we were trying to accomplish. After several months of implementing the ideas of research in practice, I began to understand better ways to define a research question and to create a baseline for research comparisons. I began to realize that I had chosen a somewhat broad area to research. It seemed that I had attempted an action research practitioner-initiated project without having clearly understood this in March 1998 when I began.

Overall, I learned about the process of research in practice from this first experience with it. However, the writing of this report extended over a great span of time, and I eventually began to understand that my project was too large for me to confidently point to conclusive patterns and results from the four activities which were observed. That is not to say that what we are doing at our campus is irrelevant to research in practice. On the contrary, I hope my description of the context and the tools used will help others. In the context in which I work, a three-year plan of introducing ideas, providing structure for learning about them, and waiting for student-initiated activities from these seeds is possibly a reasonable expectation. Elsa Auerbach (1992) describes this process in *Making meaning, making change*:

> Evidence of learning may not show up within a pre-specified time frame or at the moment it is being evaluated. It may take months after a class ends for its impact to manifest itself. (p. 21)

In closing, I would like to thank the students and other staff members, as well as the director of our campus, for patiently giving me as many opportunities as I needed to work on this project.

References

Âcimowina: Storytelling. (2000). Edmonton, AB: Voices Rising/Learning at the Centre Press.

Auerbach, E. R. (1992). *Making meaning, making change: Participatory curriculum development for adult ESL literacy.* McHenry, IL: Delta Systems.

Auerbach, E. R. (1997). The power of voices and the voices of power. Paper presented at the HCLPP Conference, Hawaii.

Cardinal, P. (1997). *The Cree People.* Edmonton, AB: Tribal Chiefs Institute of Treaty 6 and Duval House.

Courtoreille, F., & Courtoreille, M. (1997). *Roast moose and rosaries: Fred and Mary's story.* Moberly Lake, BC: Twin Sisters Publishing Company.

Hale, S. (1998). Research-in-action: Demystifying the process, a lesson learned at the very beginning. *Groundwork, 20*(1), 10–1.

Hayes, E., & Walter, P. G. (1995). A comparison of small group learning approaches in adult literacy education. *Adult Basic Education, 5* (3), 133–151.

Osborne, K. (1991). *Teaching for democratic citizenship.* Toronto, ON: Our Schools Ourselves Education Foundation.

Starting points. (1995). St. John's, NF: Cabot College.

Write now. (1993). St. John's, NF: Literacy Office.

Resource List

Kituskeenow cultural land-use and occupancy study. (1999). Calgary, AB: Arctic Institute.

LeClaire, N., & Cardinal, G. (1998). *Alberta elders' Cree dictionary.* Edmonton, AB: University of Alberta Press.

Marcuse, G. (1993). *First Nations: The circle unbroken* [Film]. (Available from the National Film Board of Canada.)

Napoleon, A. (Ed.). (1998). *Bushland spirit: Our elders speak.* Moberly Lake, BC: Twin Sisters Publishing Company.

Appendix A

Questions about *Roast moose and rosaries* June 11, 1998

Your answers can help me choose what books we read in Real Life Reading class. They can help other teachers who work with adult students choose books for their groups.

Do you know who wrote this book?

Where do the writers live?

Were you able to read and understand this book on your own?

Were you able to read and understand this book when you read out loud with a group of people?

Do you like the looks of the book? Why or why not?

Did you learn anything about the Cree people of northern BC and Alberta from reading this book?
Explain.

Did you learn new skills from reading the book? What did you learn?

Check any of the following skills you may have learned:

- ❏ how to make or do something
- ❏ new words/meanings
- ❏ how to use verbs in your writing

Did the book remind you of skills you or Elders in your community have? Explain.

Is the book about issues that are real life issues in your community? Explain.

In future, should this book be ordered for each person to keep or should we have a set in the classroom for everyone to share?

Did you talk to other people about this book?

What did you tell them about it?

Who would be interested in this book?

Can you think of ways to improve this book?

What types of end-of-chapter questions help you improve in your reading, writing and understanding?

Please list suggestions to help me make up questions for each chapter of *Roast moose and rosaries*.

May I discuss your comments with other people who teach adults in Alberta (Participatory Approaches Project)? ❑ Yes ❑ No

May I use your name with your comments? ❑ Yes ❑ No

Appendix B

Questions about *The Cree People* March 16, 1998

1.   Do you know who wrote this book?

2.   What year was it published?

3.   What is the name of the publisher?

4.   Were you interested in topics presented in the book? Give examples of topics you liked discussing.

5.   Did you learn new skills from reading the book?

    ❏   how to make or do something
    ❏   new words/meanings
    ❏   how to understand charts, graphs

6.   Do you think reading about Cree culture changes your outlook about your culture in any way?

7.   Was the reading level comfortable?

8.   Was it factual information?
Was it carefully researched?

9.   Do you like the looks of the book? Why or why not?

10.   In future, should this book be ordered for each person to keep or should it be a book kept in class for everyone to share?

11.   Do you have criticisms of the book?

    ❏   ways to improve it?
    ❏   anything missing?

May I discuss your comments with other people who teach adults in Alberta (Participatory Approaches Project)?   ❏ Yes   ❏ No

May I use your name with your comments?   ❏ Yes   ❏ No

Appendix C

Questions about the field trip

Name _____   Date _____

Level _____

Please answer the following questions if you went to the Gallery of Aboriginal Culture at the Provincial Museum on May 5.

Why did you go to the Gallery of Aboriginal Culture?

Did you learn anything about your culture?   ❏ Yes   ❏ No
Explain

Were you satisfied with the trip?   ❏ Yes   ❏ No
Explain what you liked or did not like about the trip.

Would you like to go on a day trip to somewhere in Alberta next school year?   ❏ Yes   ❏ No
Your suggestions about where to go:

Would you like to go on a two-night trip to somewhere in Alberta next school year?   ❏ Yes   ❏ No

Your suggestions about where to go:

How could we raise the money?

Would you help with fundraising for a trip?   ❏ Yes   ❏ No

May I discuss your comments with other people who teach adults in Alberta (Participatory Practices Project)?   ❏ Yes   ❏ No

May I use your name with your comments?   ❏ Yes   ❏ No

Appendix D

Questions about the Writers' Workshop

Name _____ Date _____

Level _____

Please answer the following questions if you took part in the Writers' Workshop with Larry Loyie and Constance Brissenden (May 11 to 15).

Check the session(s) which you participated in.
- ❏ Monday morning presentation by Larry and Constance
- ❏ Monday afternoon presentation by Larry and Constance

- ❏ Tuesday Block 1 Video Script Writing (Brad's group)
- ❏ Tuesday Block 2 Photo stories (BEL)

- ❏ Wednesday Block 1 Narration (High School)
- ❏ Wednesday Block 2 Oral Histories (BEL)

- ❏ Thursday Block 1 (High School)
- ❏ Thursday Block 2 Group Poem

Did you meet by yourself with Larry and Constance to discuss your writing?
- ❏ Yes ❏ No

If Yes, what did you learn about writing?

Did you participate in the Writing Jamboree on Friday morning?
- ❏ Yes ❏ No

If you were at the Writing Jamboree, check what you did:
- ❏ listened to others read
- ❏ read a story of your own
- ❏ asked someone to read your story for you
- ❏ presented a gift to the writers
- ❏ watched the video of the Writing Jamboree

What did you think of the Writing Jamboree?

What did you learn during the week of the workshop?

Would you be interested in having some type of workshop for students next school year, 1998 to 1999? ❑ Yes ❑ No

If you said Yes, what would you like to learn in a workshop?

Check your choice(s).

❑ math skills   ❑ science projects
❑ gardening in the area   ❑ traditional medicines
❑ music   ❑ art
❑ writing stories   ❑ basket making
❑ smoking fish or meat
❑ other suggestions   _____

If you would like to have another workshop, would you like to be involved in organizing it? ❑ Yes ❑ No

Do you think it is a good idea to have snack foods after the sessions?
❑ Yes ❑ No

Suggestions for types of snacks you enjoy:

May I discuss your comments with other people who teach adults in Alberta (Participatory Practices Project)? ❑ Yes ❑ No

May I use your name with your comments? ❑ Yes ❑ No

Appendix E

From an Instructor's Perspective: A Response to *The Cree People*

On March 30, 1998, *The Edmonton Journal* published the findings of a national survey involving 10,000 First Nations and Aboriginal people. Eighty per cent of those interviewed indicated a need to return to traditional ways to promote community wellness. Not only is Canada a multicultural nation, but diversity flourishes and it is important to take pride in the unique culture of an individual.

The book *The Cree People* allows this pride to be recognized. It spans the spectrum from the wisdom of elders to the struggle for identity amongst the young people—a generation of students, parents, educators and children.

The photographs, case studies, comprehensive questions and inspiring anecdotes provide an excellent resource not only for First Nations Aboriginal peoples, but for people of all cultures; also, the reading level is suited for the high school preparatory BEL program at [this college].

Especially when used in adult education where experiential learning is a critical component to instruction, the book *The Cree People* needs to be supplemented with guest speakers, videos, newspaper articles and structured discussion. The book, in this case, becomes an instrument —a framework—for discerning that unique identity that evokes pride in an individual. It kindles the spark of a journey that begins, one that needs to be encouraged by visits to museums, ceremonial rituals and a regular practice of culture in some small way.

Leslie S. Sargunaraj
March 31, 1998

Chapter 6

Changing Places: A Study About Factors That Can Affect Sharing the Facilitator's Role in a Women's Writing Group

Deborah Morgan

Deborah Morgan

Changing Places: A Study of Factors That Can Affect Sharing the Facilitator's Role in a Women's Writing Group

Introduction

I've never thought of myself as a researcher. I have always been a literacy practitioner, someone deeply involved in and committed to the day-to-day practice of promoting literacy with adult students. I thought research was an area reserved for academics in university settings, people much more learned and knowledgeable than me. For that reason, I was hesitant to get involved in the Participatory Approaches/Research in Practice Project. I'm glad I did decide to get involved, because I now know that research isn't something I need to be afraid of. Slowing down long enough to reflect on my practice was sometimes tedious, frustrating and even personally painful work. However, it was also exciting, eye-opening and worth the effort. Through my research for this project, I found important answers to questions I had about participatory literacy education, and I also learned a great deal about myself—an outcome I hadn't expected.

My research project grew out of the work I was doing to help a group of women establish a women's co-operative in Camrose. We began working on this idea when the funding for the Chapters Program, in which we had previously been involved, came to an end in June 1997.

The Chapters Program

The Chapters Program[1] was a literacy/life skills program designed by and for women receiving government financial assistance who wanted to make changes in their lives. The idea for the Chapters Program came from some women who had previously participated in an eight-month job readiness program that they felt was overly structured and "demeaning to women." The program had been an unpleasant

---

[1]The Chapters Program was funded by the National Literacy Secretariat, Human Resources Development Canada. Alberta Learning is a partner in the cost-shared national literacy program.

experience for everyone involved, myself included. I had helped coordinate the program when one of the coordinators took a maternity leave.

A few months after the job readiness program ended, I met with four "graduates" in an effort to design a program that would be more effective in meeting their needs. The women called the new program Chapters because they hoped it would help them start a new chapter in their lives.

From the very beginning, I encouraged the women in Chapters to define and take part in the details and operations of the program. It was clear that they had a better sense of what they needed than I did. Chapters grew and evolved over three years into a highly regarded, student-centred program that focused on writing as a means of exploring and documenting life experiences. The women came to enjoy writing and later published their work in a number of small publications. Their confidence and excitement about writing eventually resulted in a publication called *Writing Out Loud* (1997), a handbook of exercises and ideas to encourage students and their instructors to write and learn together. *Writing Out Loud* was eagerly received by the literacy community, provincially and nationally, which was very exciting and gratifying for the Chapters participants.

The Women's Co-operative

When the funding for Chapters ended, some of the women got together with community stakeholders (people from an addictions organization, the local literacy program, government social services and employment offices, and the local women's shelter) to talk about the idea of a women's co-operative. They openly discussed their desire to continue to build on what they had accomplished in the Chapters Program. The idea for a co-operative was well supported by everyone in attendance. Three women from Chapters, three other community members and I formed a committee to set up the LeapFrog Women's Society. The goal of the Society was to establish a women's co-operative that would be a safe meeting place, as well as providing programming and resource services for women facing the difficulties of unemployment, poor health, poverty and isolation.

When they were getting the co-operative off the ground, some of the women who had been part of the Chapters Program found they missed the time they had spent together writing. They came to me with the idea of setting up a Women's Writing Group as a program for the LeapFrog Co-op. I wasn't sure I wanted to add more to my already full

How the LeapFrog Women's Co-operative got its name

The women who formed the co-operative chose the name LeapFrog because frogs go through a transformation from egg to tadpole to immature then mature frogs. They liked the idea that they were going through a transition, too. Also, leapfrog is a game that requires more than one player. And finally, frogs can't jump backwards! It was their hope to always move forward in their lives.

plate, but at the time I was enrolled in the course component of the Participatory Approaches/Research in Practice Project. I saw that I could use what I was learning to help the women in the writing group assume responsibility for the facilitation and management of the group. A participatory approach to learning seemed to fit the co-operative model the women were working with.

I explained to the women that I hoped they would eventually be able to facilitate and operate the writing group on their own. They expressed both their uncertainty about their ability to facilitate a group and their willingness to work together to see what might happen. It seemed like a good fit for research in practice to examine the means of transferring the facilitation and ownership of a program over to the women in this writing group.

Understanding Participatory Approaches

The Chapters Program

When I look back at it now, the Chapters Program had been more participatory than I realized. I struggled often with trying to define the Chapters Program to other adult educators, since it didn't follow any traditional guideline or format. The program seemed to grow and evolve as the women became increasingly ready to take on more roles within the program and more responsibility for their own learning. As I read about participatory literacy education, I found information that described a lot of our practice in the Chapters Program. This literature provided me with a better vocabulary for defining our practice.

Hayes and Walter (1995) recognized that there are many different terms used in educational practices for which some agree on similar meanings and others consider to be totally different. "Terms like 'co-operative learning' or 'participatory education' are frequently used interchangeably, or one term is used by different authors to encompass rather different instructional approaches" (p. 134). They also recognized that there is no single best approach, but "a plurality of approaches can lend vitality to the field and accommodate diverse learner needs and program goals" (p. 134). The purpose of their article was to help clarify the confusion around certain terms. This clarification helped me to see that the Chapters Program, over time, had embraced a number of different approaches that had helped the women become more active in the program and in their learning.

Following is a description of the four types of group learning described by Hayes and Walter (1995) and how the Chapters Program utilized different group learning styles at different times.

Co-operative Learning

Co-operative learning is described as an alternative to traditional individualized learning. Used most extensively with children, co-operative learning is structured so that students work together in small groups on specific tasks. The teacher designs the group activities and maintains authority, although "the teacher serves primarily as a 'manager' and observer of group activities, not becoming involved in the groups except to intervene and teach skills if needed" (pp. 136–137). The authors also state that "involving students in co-operative learning provides them with an alternative method of learning and potentially increases their interactions with other students, but does not necessarily democratize the classroom" (p. 137).

The women attending the Chapters Program had not done well in school. They rebelled against authority, felt they didn't fit in and often didn't have many friends in school. The first task of the Chapters Program was to create a safe place for people to be and learn, unlike the traditional learning settings the women had previously experienced. The women then had to learn about co-operation—that even though they had different personal and academic issues, they would have to learn to work together to be able to benefit from the program. Co-operative learning was a first step to that end. Not many of the women had been in a positive group setting before; some had not worked in a group setting at all, so it took some time for them to see past themselves as individuals. We worked on small projects together (such as making collages to decorate the classroom) to promote teamwork and an understanding of what it meant to co-operate with one another.

Collaborative Learning

The role of the teacher is different again in collaborative learning. Hayes and Walter (1995) state:

> The teacher participates as a member of the "learning community"; thus, teachers as well as learners can be considered collaborators in the group learning process. The

teacher still has primary responsibility for designing the learning activities, presumably drawing on the self-identified needs and backgrounds of the learners. (p. 138)

As the women became more comfortable in the Chapters Program, they began to identify specific interests and topics that they wanted to learn more about. One woman brought a magazine article into class about menopause, because she was curious about symptoms and treatment. After some discussion about medical terminology and female anatomy, the group encouraged her to see a doctor (something she hadn't done in eight years) and to have a mammogram. With the support of the group, she carried through with their suggestions and was able to report back to the group about the experience and what she learned.

On a beautiful warm day, one of the women wrote in her freewriting that she wished we could go outside and write. I couldn't see any reason why we couldn't, so the next day we brought blankets and snacks and set up our classroom in the park. We lay on blankets and wrote about how good it felt to be in the fresh air.

As the women identified issues and areas of interest to them, I did my best to help them find information they needed, provide relevant learning experiences, and incorporate their ideas into our everyday learning. The students worked well together and enjoyed (and benefited from) this non-traditional, non-threatening approach to learning. I called this "real life literacy." I described our program to others as one that encouraged students to be actively involved in their own learning, which was perhaps another way to describe collaborative learning.

Hayes and Walter (1995) also describe collaborative learning as an approach that suggests that literacy is a social activity—that "becoming literate involves not only the acquisition of discrete skills, but a broader understanding of the social norms and practice that is associated with use of language skills, as well as the socially constructed nature of knowledge" (p. 137). This was certainly true in the Chapters classroom. The women had great fun together and created a strong community and support network for themselves, in the classroom as well as in their everyday lives. When one of the women mentioned that she had an overabundance of rhubarb in her garden, the women asked if we could take some time off to make pies. Instead of "taking time off," we took our classroom to my kitchen and spent an afternoon baking pies, sharing and comparing recipes, and talking about how to read cookbooks and convert imperial measurements to the metric system.

Participatory Learning

As I read about participatory learning, I realized that many (but not all) of the students in the Chapters Program had moved from group collaboration to greater personal participation. Hayes and Walter (1995) state that

> participatory education, as the name suggests, seeks to promote the active participation of adult learners in designing, organizing, managing and evaluating literacy education programs. In participatory literacy education, the concept of literacy is extended beyond language skills and practices to the ability of learners to take more control over their lives and learning. (p. 139)

In the Chapters Program, students were involved in identifying and designing learning activities; their ideas for program improvement and development were valued and integrated into the program wherever possible. They were involved in the program, but not to the point of managing it or having control of it. This was never an objective of the program, and yet I now see that it would have been possible.

One example that comes to mind is when the women got together and approached me about changing the hours of the program. They wanted to start at 9:30 am instead of 9:00 am to give them more time to get their children ready for school. And they wanted to end the day at 3:00 pm instead of 3:30 pm so that they could pick their children up or be at home to greet them after school. This was something I hadn't thought of, even though I knew it was important to honour the women as mothers. It was an easy decision to change the schedule. I realize now that at that time it was still my decision to make.

Further reading on group learning and participatory education practices revealed that many educators view participatory education as a means of effecting social change. Cranton (1996) refers to participatory education as transformative group learning. Cranton believes that the process of moving toward transformative or participatory group learning "is collaborative, but it goes beyond mutual understanding and has a goal to effect change, either individually or socially" (p. 30). I began to think about and remember the number of women in the Chapters Program who had undergone personal changes that allowed them to transform the world around them. In particular, two women chose to leave abusive relationships and become physically and emotionally more independent. Learning about family violence, receiving support from the group and identifying their personal determination to make things better helped them make this choice.

The Women's Co-operative

I could see that the Women's Writing Group at the LeapFrog Co-operative had an even greater potential to become a participatory program. Most of the women were already accustomed to a collaborative approach to learning. They were at a point where they wanted to make changes in their lives. Through the LeapFrog Co-operative, they hoped to become more skilled and independent. They hoped that the local community would come to view them, and all women, with more respect. I was comfortable with the idea that group learning could be seen as a social activity as well as a means of promoting personal and social change. I had learned a great deal about collaborative and participatory learning through the Chapters Program and looked forward to working with the women in the Women's Writing Group and the LeapFrog Co-operative in developing and establishing a program that would be managed more by the participants than by an instructor or organizer.

The Women's Writing Group

The women who came together to write agreed that the immediate goal of the Women's Writing Group was to use writing as a non-threatening way to get thoughts and ideas on paper and a way to talk about and validate their life experiences. The women in the writing group and other community members established a Mission Statement for the LeapFrog Women's Co-operative that read:

> We are a co-operative women's group which offers life enhancing activities to women and their families in a safe and welcoming environment. Formed on a secure grassroots foundation, the LeapFrog Women's Co-operative is a model for individuals and groups who wish to work and learn together, and have a proactive voice and credible presence in the community.

I viewed taking part in the activities of the writing group as an opportunity for the co-op members to strengthen their working relationship and build on the mission of the co-operative. The writing group was the first official program of the LeapFrog Women's Co-operative, so it was hoped that it would be a successful model for future programs, demonstrating a need for ongoing funding. I believed that a participatory approach to work and learning would give the women some of the tools they needed to reach their goals.

From February to June, 1998, the writing group met two afternoons a week from 1:00 pm to 3:00 pm at the new LeapFrog Women's Co-operative facility—a bay in a strip mall in downtown Camrose. There was space there for us to make coffee and sit together at a large table. Six women attended the group on a regular basis, and another four women came and went over the five months we worked together. Of the six regulars, one was married, two were in relationships and three were single. The women ranged in age from 28 to 53 years. Three of the women had young children and the others had children who were older and/or away from home. Four of the women had known each other previously (through Chapters and 12 Step program support groups) and two were new to the group. Although they were at different levels of literacy, all of the women were comfortable with writing.

All of the women had experience with substance abuse and physical and emotional abuse, and most of the women had health problems ranging from painful back injuries to bouts of severe depression. Even though I had more years of education and paid employment, some of my experiences had not been dissimilar to the group's. Newly divorced from an alcoholic husband, I was on my own raising two teenage boys. I also live with the challenges of multiple sclerosis. Because of our shared backgrounds, our desire to write, our respect for one another as women and our commitment to the idea of the LeapFrog Women's Co-operative, we got along well and enjoyed spending time together.

Each time we met, we would start the afternoon with five minutes of freewriting, as had been our practice in the Chapters Program. This is a timed exercise in which everyone in the group writes for five minutes about anything that comes to mind. This is a way to get centred and feel focused for further writing. Reading authors such as Elaine Farris Hughes was increasing my awareness of the powerful effects of writing. I saw writing as an especially good way to help the women build confidence in themselves and in their ability to learn. Hughes (1992) says:

> Nobody can write what you can write. You are one of a kind and have had one-of-a-kind experiences. And, on top of that, nobody else sees or feels exactly what you see and feel. Right this very minute, you've got enough material stored within you to write a shelf full of books . . . I'm convinced that most people are born storytellers and that the act of writing can be a pleasure. It can be your recreation, your job, your friend, your teacher. To sum it up, I believe in writing. I think the act of writing can change lives and save souls. I've seen it happen. (p. 3)

Following the freewriting, the group members read their writing out loud to one another. This gave everyone a chance to be heard and to get a sense of how the rest of the group was feeling. After freewriting, we normally did writing activities around issues that were important to the group members, such as children, family, garage sales, independence and security. The women identified topics or brought ideas they had read about in a magazine or heard on television. Using a collaborative approach, I would help them to design writing exercises that would provide them with the opportunity to talk and write about their ideas, ask questions and learn from one another.

When I thought about our writing group this morning, I was very excited. Different thoughts went through my head. I imagined myself freewriting back on the first day of Chapters. I was nervous and felt like a kid on the first day of class. I was afraid of being laughed at, at the things I wrote. I imagined everyone else there writing with big words I knew I wouldn't understand. As it turned out, I was accepted for who I was, what I wrote and how I wrote. (Sharron)

Questions, Questions and More Questions

Our effort to share the facilitating role began with the facilitation of the daily freewriting activity. We talked about how to facilitate the steps of timing the writing, asking members to read their writing aloud and then giving feedback to each writer. As the group grew comfortable with the idea, the women took turns being the freewriting facilitator. As well, I encouraged everyone to bring in their own writing ideas or topics, which, as their comfort and confidence continued to grow, they did. It felt like all the components and possibilities for a well-functioning participatory program were there, but for some reason, it wasn't working.

Every day the writing group met was different. Each meeting seemed to present new challenges, for me as well as for the students. All of us had to change our way of thinking about the roles we normally played in a learning setting. I struggled constantly with when and how to let go as a facilitator, and the students struggled with the responsibility of taking on more leadership within the group. I was still facilitating long after I thought I would be able to take a back seat. Some days went well, others didn't, and I was left wondering why things were not going well, especially since we had all agreed that having members take more leadership in the facilitation of the group was what we wanted.

I was full of questions:

- What made one day go so smoothly when just two days before, nothing seemed to work?

- Why aren't the women participating more, when that is what they had indicated they wanted?

- Why is it that the women are willing to participate one day, but not the next?

- Why am I having trouble letting go of the responsibility for facilitating the group?

- How do I help the students to trust this process when I'm not entirely sure about it myself?

- What, exactly, does it mean to participate? Are my expectations too high?

I couldn't put my finger on what was wrong. I was quick (as many of us are) to question my own abilities: "Maybe I'm too focused on control to be able to let go." "Maybe I'm not experienced enough to implement a more participatory approach in a learning setting." "Maybe I'm not being an effective teacher or a strong enough encourager."

Looking for Answers

My research mentor listened to my frustrations and encouraged me to keep notes about the daily events in the classroom. She thought that over time I would be able to identify factors that were influencing the progress of the group. I began to keep a journal of my thoughts and feelings about what I was learning. I tried to write in my journal after each class with the writing group. As well, at the end of each class, I often asked the women how they felt about the writing group and about their participation in the process. I kept notes during these discussions.

The journal and discussions helped me step back from the Women's Writing Group and my involvement within the group. I wanted to see the big picture more objectively, instead of feeling so emotionally involved. It was only then that I began to see the reasons for some of our setbacks.

Learning about the reasons for setbacks became my research interest, and eventually I narrowed my many questions down to one: "What factors influence the process of sharing the facilitator's role in a women's writing group?"

Five of the six women who regularly attended the writing group agreed to take part in the research and were comfortable with my using their first names in research documentation. They also agreed that I could include their freewriting as a research source. Those who participated were Alice, Jenna, Sharron, Barb and Stephanie. I didn't have the women sign formal consent forms regarding the use of their comments or ideas, but checked with them on an ongoing basis to make sure I was accurately portraying their thoughts and feelings.

I continued to keep a journal and notes about the after-class discussions. As well, two students involved in participatory projects at The Learning Centre in Edmonton came to Camrose to interview the women about their participation in the writing group. I was away at a meeting on the day they came. The interview was videotaped to include in a presentation about participatory approaches at a provincial literacy conference. With the women's permission, I was able to use a copy of the videotape as an additional source of information in my research. One of the women transcribed the tape for me.

As my research progressed, I found there were a number of gaps in my data. To get more specific information, I drew up a questionnaire for the women to fill out and return to me. I typed their answers and collated the responses.

Exploring the Data

I had no idea that doing my data analysis would be such a lengthy and intricate part of my research. Altogether, I had five sources of information—my journal, the discussion notes, the video transcript, participants' freewriting and the questionnaire. When it came time to pull my data together, I discovered I had bits of paper and ideas all over the place—in my notebook, on the computer, on sheets of paper and in my head. I didn't know how to begin to organize all the information I had.

I learned the art of cutting and pasting information onto file cards. I surveyed my notes and clipped out paragraphs that I thought were particularly relevant to the question I was trying to answer. I coded the clippings by colour to identify whether they were from my journal, discussion notes or questionnaires, so that I could go back to the context if I needed to.

Working with smaller pieces of information on file cards was less daunting than working with the piles of papers I had accumulated. After shuffling the cards around and organizing them into groups of connected ideas, I was able to see trends or similarities in my observations. My experiences with the writing group and insights from the literature I had been reviewing about participatory approaches in literacy education helped me identify patterns. I could see the importance of the information I had gathered on topics such as "building trust," "group dynamics" and "the role of the instructor." As I continued to work with the women in the group and focus on my research, some categories became more intriguing than others.

As I began to draw conclusions from my research and document my findings for this paper, I asked the women for their feedback on my notes. I called this a member check. Each of the women spoke to me individually and I noted their comments. I felt I needed to begin writing about my findings even though the direction wasn't perfectly clear. Writing about and around the data was cathartic for me; it felt good to be working with and relating my experiences to the research data in a more systematic way.

Finding Some Answers

As I worked with the data I had collected, I could see different factors that influenced the group members' efforts to participate in the group by facilitating writing exercises. The group's initial excitement with ownership of the process waned as realities of life continued to be top priority. There were also factors that influenced my enthusiasm and ability to give over that ownership.

Weather

As an example, something as mundane as weather had a dramatic effect on our moods, our health and our mobility. A number of times we made plans to do something new on a certain day, and when that day came, it was cold and dreary and everyone's spirits were down.

> It's so hard to get the baby around when it's cold and snowy. And now she's really sick with a cold. I always seem to get sick when she does. I wish the sun would come out. I don't feel much like writing today. (Jenna)

Thank goodness the weather wasn't always dreary! Meeting from February to June, we had the pleasure of working together through the coming of spring as well as the last of the winter storms. I always noticed more energy and enthusiasm in the group on warm, bright afternoons.

Personal health

Another everyday reality that affected people's interest and willingness to participate in the group was their health. When people felt well, they were able to take risks and have fun with their learning, and on days that they weren't well, they were withdrawn and less comfortable with participating.

> *When I'm depressed I don't even like to go out of the house. I can't concentrate so it's hard to do my work. Sometimes I'm here in body but not in mind.* (Alice)

Some of the group members had on-going health problems that were a real frustration for them.

> *On the days I'm not feeling well I have a hard time participating in the group. Sometimes I ache so much I can't think at all, my mind just goes blank. When the weather's bad I really ache. I have to take a lot of medication and I think it affects my memory. But when I'm feeling well, I'm very eager to take part and my mind is much more open to ideas. I still like to attend class when I'm not feeling well, to get what I can from that day but I sure hope it doesn't affect the people in the class the days I don't feel well.* (Sharron)

The members of the group were caring and sympathetic when someone was ill, but they would (often unknowingly) let another's illness affect their own feelings of well-being.

> *When someone is down, it's hard for me to concentrate. I get depressed about what the person is feeling. I think the whole group cares so much about each other it's hard not to get emotional if one of us is down.* (Alice)

There were times when my own health problems surfaced, but on one particular occasion, this was a good thing. A couple of months after the group really got going, I had to go into the hospital. I worried that the group would have trouble without me, but my being away had the opposite effect.

> I'm so pleased that the women decided to keep meeting even though I'm not there. Stephanie said when she visited that they had a great day today. Barb led the freewriting and they spent

most of the afternoon writing and talking about having babies. I wasn't sure they could manage, but obviously they can manage just fine. I'm a little ashamed that I doubted their ability. (my journal)

We each had to deal with our own physical and emotional health problems, our feelings about our health and our interactions with the group. I know we all did our best to stay well and feel well, but it was a rare day that we all felt well at the same time.

The weather and our health were contributing factors to the day-to-day productiveness of the group, but there were some much bigger issues. I identified a trend in my research data I called group dynamics. I started to see the complexities that can arise in trying to encourage more participation within a group.

Group Dynamics

I've been thinking today how, as basic literacy instructors, we are often asked to work with people who are dealing with very difficult realities in their lives. We (students and instructor) are put in a room together with some who want to be there and others who don't. Most have had negative experiences with learning and have a fear of repeating past failures. The truth is, most are afraid of success because it is so unfamiliar. There are introverts and extroverts in the group and each group member has her own learning style (which she is probably quite unaware of). Some of the group members take an immediate dislike to each other, some buddy up right away and others feel isolated because of their cultural backgrounds. Not many are able to identify their feelings, let alone communicate them to a group or instructor. This is my reality as an instructor. My hope is that we can learn to get along and work together as we are learning together. Sometimes the learning is much less complex than the dynamics of the group. (my journal)

It was obvious that before I was able to encourage the women to take a more active role in the writing group, I had to allow time for the group to establish itself. This process seemed to take a long time. It was difficult to find any information that spoke of how to establish a participatory learning group. As I tried to understand how and why people were interacting the way they were, I drew a lot on a Life Skills Coaches Training program I had taken a couple of years ago. When I pulled out the resources from that course, I was surprised and somewhat comforted by how accurately the description of group dynamics related to what I was seeing in the Women's Writing Group.

Resources from the Toronto YWCA (1982) suggest that a small group is an excellent environment in which to acquire "the skills of relating and interacting with others. . . . It is the membership [in a small group] which gives rise to problems" (p. 35). The resource suggests that to achieve membership in a group, a person must meet three interpersonal needs; namely, inclusion, affection and control. In my notes and findings about group dynamics, I could see how important these interpersonal needs were.

Inclusion

> [Inclusion is] the need for a sense of belonging with others; the need to be included. Inclusion is expressed in the need to attract the attention and interest of others and to be a member of the group, yet a distinct and unique person within it. (YWCA, 1982, p. 35)

It was important for members of the group to feel included, and yet their life circumstances made it difficult for them to attend regularly. When they missed an afternoon of writing, they felt left out and we felt like we were back at square one of establishing a comfortable working group. It was especially difficult when someone stopped coming to the group. I felt disappointed when people left the group. The others in the group had similar feelings, but may have been better than I was at accepting other's choices.

> *I feel bad that she is going to miss out on so much. But I have to focus my mind on my own forward movement.* (Alice)

> *Everyone has a right to make their own decision. I believe in letting go of something that isn't good for me.* (Sharron)

When our numbers decreased, I felt some responsibility for encouraging new membership. The original group members agreed that having more people in the writing group was a good idea, but they found adjusting to changes in group dynamics wasn't easy.

> *It's hard because we have a safe environment before the new person starts, then we have to start over feeling comfortable as a group again. I'm a little wary of the new person's motive. My environment is invaded by an alien! Maybe I'm jealous that the attention is on them. (Silly, I know.) But I want them to feel good about themselves so it's OK.* (Alice)

I always stand guard and feel that person out. I can usually tell by my instincts if I'm going to bond with that new person in a couple of days. If I don't feel trust I stay my distance yet always try to support them. (Sharron)

When someone new joined the group, time was required for them to feel comfortable. Jenna talked about wanting/needing to feel included:

It's hard for me sometimes because you guys all know each other. You talk about things that I don't know about. I always want to ask questions but I don't want to take up too much time doing that. I feel like I'm intruding.

Although group dynamics are always complex, they may be more so when participatory approaches are introduced into a learning setting that involves writing. The feeling of safety and inclusion within a writing group has to be particularly strong so that students are able to feel comfortable and supported as they risk personal and academic exposure through their writing.

I need to know that the people around me are about the same as me. That we'll all be treated the same. I need to know my surroundings are stress free and safe. I like a positive atmosphere to work in. I need a reason to laugh and feel good about what I'm participating in. (Alice)

Alice mentions the importance of both her physical and emotional safety. All of the women in the writing group had experienced abuse in their lives, so safety was of particular importance to them. Feeling safe also requires comfort with one's own abilities.

I'm really seeing how group dynamics plays an important role in the group's interest to participate more. They have to feel comfortable with the facilitator, comfortable with each other and also comfortable with themselves. It's all about self-esteem. They need to believe that they can do it, that they are capable. That understanding can only come with time, and support from the other participants and the facilitator. (my journal)

To feel included in a group, one has to feel like an accepted member of the group. The women were slow to trust one another (and themselves) so the group was slow to develop into the safe place it needed to be for people to feel comfortable. Trust building between the members of a group can be very difficult, especially for people who have had their trust broken in the past. Building trust also takes time. Brookfield (1995) says:

Coming to trust another person is the most fragile of human projects. It requires knowing someone over a period of time and seeing their honesty modeled in their actions. (p. 26)

The Women's Writing Group was slow to develop into an inclusive, accepting group because we weren't together often enough as a group to give trust building the time it needed.

I'm hearing how important it is to build trust with a group—especially a group of women who are being asked to write and talk about themselves—*and* be part of a research study! Meeting two afternoons a week for two hours has not given us a lot of time to build that trust. (discussion notes)

Affection

[Affection is] the need to feel close, to feel personal involvement, and to feel that one is in emotional communication with another. The affection need is expressed by giving and receiving; its workings can be seen in both attraction and aversion between individuals in the group. Some deal with this need by being equally friendly to all others or by being aloof from all. (YWCA, 1982, p. 35)

With trust comes a confidence and security that makes learning more possible and pleasurable. Feeling the affection and acceptance of others in the group is also a key to feeling comfortable with participating in a group setting.

It's therapeutic for me (to be in the writing group because it's OK to be who I am. I'm aware that others are here too, and they're with me and for me. (Stephanie)

I love being here. I don't feel lonely when I'm here. Everyone listens to me when I say something and I know I'm not being laughed at. That's a big change for me. (Alice)

Control

[Control is] the need for control over others and the need to be controlled. The control need can be observed as a continuum in the decision-making process among people. It involves power, authority and influence. Control needs within the group are usually resolved by the establishment of a 'pecking order'; this order changes from day to day but serves as a kind of baseline from which modifications are made. (YWCA, 1982, p. 35)

The mood and behaviour of each individual often had a profound effect on the rest of the group. There were a few days, especially earlier in the project, when a group member was unhappy or angry and aggressive, and her frustration often manifested in a need to control. The group was small enough that any difficult behaviour was disruptive.

I don't like it when someone tries to dominate the group. I like it when we all feel equal. When we all feel we have a chance to contribute. (Alice)

I get frustrated when others are having a bad day, yet I still feel supportive. But when someone is talking too much or being loud or not paying attention, I lose concentration and then I can't write well. (Sharron)

The anger and frustrations group members brought to class with them were most often around difficult circumstances in their personal lives. Stephanie wrote about her frustrations because of the lack of control in her life:

It's really hard to be here every time I'm supposed to be at the same time that I'm trying to get my life straightened out. I have to move in a month and I can't find anyone with a truck to help me. I get really mad sometimes that I'm left alone with all this stuff to do myself. Why can't Gina's dad help out once in a while? I think I need to just sit here and rest for awhile. (Stephanie)

Sometimes, because of their personal problems, the students would choose not to come to class. So much of the group process was dependent on the group members actually being there. I found it difficult to ask someone to facilitate a portion of the class when there was only one other person in the classroom.

There were only two people in the writing group today. I thought we might cancel the class, but Alice said, "Can't we still write together?" I am so conscious of the "group" doing things together, that I guess I felt we weren't effective if we weren't a whole group. As it turned out, we had a really good talk and were able to do some valuable writing. I think keeping the class going, even with one participant, certainly builds the feeling among members that I am serious about my commitment. I guess I would like them to be more serious about their commitment and attend more regularly. (discussion notes)

It was frustrating (and fascinating) for all of us to ride the group dynamics roller coaster—always trying to sort out the emotions, actions and reactions of others, while trying to find the place that we ourselves fit within the group. There were days that we felt like a team, and other days when there was almost no interaction among group members.

Looking at the different types of learning, Hayes and Walter (1995) state,

> In contrast to co-operative learning and similar to collaborative approaches, participatory literacy education does not specify the instructional activities necessary to teach group skills, but often appears to assume that these skills will emerge with the development of group identity and purpose. (p. 140)

I found that we were most productive when we were aware and considerate of the dynamics happening within the group.

Letting Go—An Attempt to Put Theory into Practice

I struggled with two things while helping to establish our participatory program: knowing how and when to let go of my role as facilitator and knowing how to let go of the control I had when I was in the facilitator role. I struggled with the role I was supposed to play, especially when it seemed to me that members of the group were at such different stages of readiness to take on more leadership within the group.

> I can see that letting go changes from day to day. Some days the students are very independent and some days not at all. And some days one student is independent and others not, and the next day that can change totally. Judging the mood of the group can be very difficult. How do you work with a group that has some members who want you to step back and others who want you to teach? What happens to the group dynamics in this situation? Do those who are ready resent those who are not, and vice versa? (my journal)

One day I asked the students to write about how they thought I was doing with letting go and giving more responsibility and leadership to the group. Stephanie had this to say:

> *I think that with anything, habit can be formed. Deborah has been in the role of facilitator for a long time, so it is understandable that it is second nature for her to wear the facilitator hat. As soon as the project moved towards having student facilitation, Deborah was very eager to participate as a fellow student. It was like watching someone who was trying to correct a speech habit—she would correct herself facilitating and was honest and even apologetic about "taking charge." She says it's sometimes hard to let go.*

Stephanie was right, I did find it hard. As always, I was full of questions.

> I think that moving from a teacher role to a facilitator role in a participatory program can bring out feelings of guilt and neglect for the instructor. Maybe it's part of letting go, but it's painful and difficult. As an instructor, I feel like I'm setting people up for failure. I know that if I'm doing my job right (i.e., helping to prepare people to take charge), that won't happen. But some students are so glad of the freedom, they grab it without thinking and then can't manage. And others feel pushed and then experience increased anxiety. How do you know when someone is ready to get more involved in their own learning? (my journal)

Through Sharron's and Alice's response to the question, I learned that I wasn't giving them enough opportunity to do their own letting go of me as the instructor. I wasn't fostering readiness and independence.

> *I find that hosting freewriting is giving me responsibility that is just great. But as long as Deborah is in the same room, I'll always use her as a crutch. I can't seem to take charge completely in her presence although I'm getting better.* (Sharron)

> *In this participatory writing workshop, Deborah has let us take charge. We have had some advice on how to facilitate our freewriting. She has been very good to let us run the show, so to speak. Today she totally forgot to let one of us facilitate. I think it was because Sharron brought a guest. We all figured it was her turn anyway, and of course it was so natural, none of us went ahead and said, "Whose turn is it today to do the freewriting?" We like to facilitate, but it was nice to have Deborah there. For me, I would rather have her do it. I've only volunteered once so I haven't had a lot of practice yet.* (Alice)

It was hard to hear this about myself. Sharron said that I was the group's crutch. I wanted to be a support, but in a healthy way. A mentor, an encourager, but not a crutch. I could see I was doing some things right, but that I still had a lot of learning to do.

> None of this is easy. It's exhausting. As teachers we're required to be honest, clear in our beliefs, flexible to students' needs, always willing to reflect on our thinking. So many skills, some of them learned, some of them inherent. I don't know if I'm equipped to do this. (my journal)

Influencing others

One of the first writing ideas that one of the students brought into the classroom was to write a letter to Oprah. The idea came from Barb:

> *I guess I mentioned Oprah because I saw a show where she talked about literacy and she has a book club so I thought they would be interested in what we would have to say. Here we are from the little town of Camrose and people have written in to her from Canada before. Even if we don't go on the show, that doesn't matter. That really wasn't the reason. I'm sure we'll hear from her, though. I had always dreamt about doing something like this myself, but I was too scared to. [Writing to Oprah about our Women's Writing Group] was something I thought of off the top of my head and the group kind of grabbed on to it.* (video interview)

The students grabbed on to the idea, but I was hesitant. I was concerned about what the true purpose in writing to Oprah was.

> What do you do when you are trying to promote a participatory project and you aren't comfortable with the direction the group is going? The women in the writing group have decided to write to Oprah. I have some real ethical concerns about this. I realize a lot of this is my own stuff—I don't have a high regard for talk shows, although I respect the work Oprah has done. And I'm worried about the expectations the group has. Even though they continue to downplay it, there is an underlying hope that they will be invited to be guests on Oprah's show. I'm not sure what the true intentions for writing to Oprah are. I keep hoping it's because they want to promote the idea of writing, not the idea of their winning a trip to Chicago. I'm not really sure why I'm so uncomfortable with this, but I am. But they're excited about it and working well together, so I have to keep telling myself to stop worrying and stop being so judgemental. (my journal)

In the end, through a strong group effort, the women put together a package of information for Oprah that they were very proud of. What started as a simple idea to write a letter, became a unique and well-presented folder of personal photographs, biographies and ideas about why writing is important. (Barb had even found an article in *LIFE Magazine* about Oprah that stated that she loved to read but was uncomfortable with writing.) I had to admit, I was impressed. I was just as excited as everyone else on the day the envelope went into the mailbox. Through this experience, the women worked together to design and carry out an activity that they felt good about. The group shaped what the end product looked like. I'm glad now that I didn't step in and stop the process because of my own personal bias and discomfort. If I had, I would have robbed the women of a valuable learning experience.

The letter to Oprah was mailed June 17th. We wrote our predictions as to Oprah's response and sealed them in an envelope. By September, when we hadn't heard from Oprah, we opened the envelope and laughed at how sure we had been that she would respond right away. It was interesting to note how Barb had changed her thinking and expectations about being on the Oprah Show and how the rest of us had found ourselves caught up in the excitement about a possible invitation to Chicago. And I was surprised when I saw how much I had been influenced by the thinking of the others in the group.

Alice: We will get a letter back from her studio people that she personally got our book and biographies. She is interested in the Canadian women who sent her information on writing. Maybe she will have her staff book us for her show and do free writing with her audience. Wishful thinking. Maybe she'll send us journals or something. I hope we hear on July 13th—my birthday.

Deborah: I think Oprah will be impressed. Maybe not impressed enough to invite us on to her show, but I think that we'll hear something more than just a thank you from some employee who is just hired to write thank you letters. I have this real positive feeling of "Go Girls"! I think we'll hear by July 5th.

Jenna: We'll get a "thank you, we've received your letter" by the end of August.

Sharron: I predict that Oprah will contact us to be on her show sometime in the near future. I predict all of us will be invited and that we'll hear by the end of August.

Barb: I predict we will get a reply thanking us for our interest and a few short words of response. I think we will hear by the middle of July.

Stephanie: I think that we will get a letter from Oprah thanking us for our stuff and that she has changed her mind about her writing abilities. My intuition says that we will hear by August 24th.

I found an e-mail address on Oprah's web page and we sent a message to her staff to make sure Oprah had received our package. This is the response we got:

Thank you for your recent e-mail to Oprah Winfrey. This is just a quick note to let you know that your message has been received.

Unfortunately, due to the overwhelming amount of mail that Ms. Winfrey is receiving, she regrets that it is impossible to answer each and every message personally. You can be sure, however, that we do read every single message.

We appreciate hearing from you and hope to see you again soon at http://www.oprah.com !

Sincerely,
The Oprah.com Staff

Taking charge

A couple of months after the Women's writing group got started, Mary Norton, a coordinator at The Learning Centre in Edmonton suggested the idea of having a group from The Centre drive out to Camrose for a visit. The women in the writing group were pleased to host the visit. The plan was for Mary to bring the students for lunch and an afternoon of writing. The following two entries from my discussion notes describe what happened.

March 19th

Made plans today for the women from The Learning Centre to come. Stephanie is going to do freewriting, Sharron the "I see, I feel" exercise, and Alice, "Writing is . . . " I think they'll do just fine. We did some practising with the group and it all went well. The students really seem to like the idea of having visitors. They are willing to really try hard about this. It's sort of the first thing they've seemed "together" about. We have some concerns about the writing level of the visitors, but everyone seems to feel comfortable about being flexible and adaptable.

March 25th

Today we had a chance to debrief about The Learning Centre visit and I sure learned a lot. In preparation for Mary's students' visit, the women had agreed to facilitate a number of different writing exercises. The students practised with our own group and I thought were all set to teach the writing exercises with the students from The Learning Centre. But a half hour before Mary arrived, they started to back out. They said they were nervous, shy, self-conscious, not feeling well, not up to it. I tried to encourage them (and I'm usually pretty good at that) but once the discussion started about being afraid, the downward spiral had started and there wasn't much

I could do. I was really disappointed because I had wanted to "show off" the students' ability to lead and participate.

So I ended up doing most of the facilitating. I found myself "taking charge" because I was afraid things were going to fall apart if I didn't. I learned today how much of that was my own stuff—wanting to show Mary that I was doing a good job with helping to establish a participatory program. The students said today that 15 minutes into the two groups working together, they felt much more comfortable and would like to have been more involved. Sharron commented, "If I'd known that the women from The Learning Centre were just like us, I would have been able to do the writing exercise myself." And Barb said, "I don't know if I could have done the teaching part, but I could have helped by writing on the flip chart." I tried to ease their fears on Thursday, but until they were able to "see for themselves" they weren't able to hear me.

They had been so definite about their decisions not to lead the group that it didn't occur to me that they might change their minds 15 minutes into the class. I think I was so busy trying to hold things together that I didn't notice how relaxed they had become and didn't take that as a sign of their "readiness." (discussion notes)

What happened on the day of The Learning Centre visit also made me look at the question of shyness. Were the students really shy, or did they feel (and act) shy because of their lack of confidence in their place in this situation? Campbell (1996) observes that

> students' shyness or fear of speech may come from past experiences where, as working class, nonacademic people, they were not heard because they did not speak the dominant language of academics and professionals such as doctors, teachers and social workers. (p. 112)

Campbell also suggests that "together, educators and students need to analyze the roots of silence, rather than attributing it to shyness or a lack of confidence" (p. 141). The last paragraph of my notes from that day relates to Campbell's observations.

> The students learned a lot from this experience as well. They admitted that their shyness was really their fear of being judged (unfairly) by people they had never met before. They admitted that they had assumed too much, that they in fact had nothing to be shy about. We talked a lot about self-confidence and trusting in our own abilities (my own

included!). It was a great discussion and should help us all when there is a "next time." (discussion notes)

Adjusting to Change—Sharing Control

It was a big change for me to let go of being a facilitator, and an equally difficult change for the students to take a stronger leadership role within the group. We were all surprised by that; we thought it would be much easier. It was quite uncomfortable for all of us to watch each other struggle with our changing roles in the classroom. Unfortunately, we never really got the chance to fully experience and get used to our new roles, as the writing group ended before we had fully recognized the learning we needed to do. Both letting go and taking charge require a new set of skills and level of confidence that take some practice.

> I never liked the idea of having control in a classroom, but neither do I feel comfortable with seeing things out of control. I've discovered a discomfort with disorganization that I didn't realize I had. I have found myself feeling guilty for taking responsibility in the classroom and guilty when I didn't. I seem to have found a rhythm with the step-forward step-back dance now that I'm more at ease with and have hopefully suffered the worst of the letting-go growing pains. (my journal)

When I asked the students what personal steps they would have to take to feel more ready to facilitate a writing class on their own, Sharron said:

> *I need more practice speaking in public. I know what I want to say and hope in time I will be better at speaking in front of a group. As long as I have guidance, I feel confident.*

Alice also talked about needing to feel more confident:

> *For me, I have to be well prepared. If I have notes on what to say and I have them with me, I'm OK. I have to be more sure of myself. I'm always afraid of doing something wrong and letting the group down. I feel more at ease working as a team in being part of a program. I don't want to run it. Maybe it's a little insecurity with myself yet.*

As an educator, I could see that I needed more practice and more confidence as well. I was reminded of this when I again read Cranton's (1996) essay on types of group learning.

It is much easier to write about the educator's roles in transformative group learning than it is to implement them in practice. Most of us feel discomfort in giving up position power, for example, and we worry about the reactions of colleagues or program administrators to our unorthodox approach to teaching. To become a truly equal participant in the group process is to feel vulnerable as an educator. Perhaps the roles evolve best with confidence in what one is doing and experience in doing it well. (p. 31)

Even at the end of the time the Women's Writing Group worked together, we still felt some confusion about our roles in the classroom. We were, however, able to talk openly about what had been difficult for us and what we still needed or wanted to work on. We wished we could have more time to adjust to and define our changing roles, but we also felt that we had learned a lot about ourselves that would help us participate more fully and appropriately in future group work.

Recommendations for Practice

I am still full of questions about myself and my practice as I write this paper. My experience in promoting a participatory approach to learning still feels raw and awkward. I did, however, learn some things that I feel would be of value for others to consider in doing similar work.

Need for Critical Reflection

Perhaps my most valuable learning from being involved in this research project was coming to understand the need for critical reflection around our practices. I always loved being part of the late-night talks literacy workers had about their experiences, successes and frustrations when they got together at a conference. Most of us worked independently in our own communities, which meant that opportunities to get together and really talk about our practices were rare. I didn't realize then that sitting in hotel rooms in our pajamas talking late into the night was actually a time of critical reflection. All I knew was those times were really valuable and very important to me.

Now, as I work through new learning situations I recognize more clearly how important critical reflection is. Brookfield (1995) outlines some of the benefits of a more reflective practice:

[Critical reflection] embeds not only our actions but also our sense of who we are as teachers in an examined reality. We know why we believe what we believe. A critically reflective teacher is much better placed to communicate to colleagues and students—as well as to herself—the rationale behind her practice. She works from a position of informed commitment. She knows why she does what she does, why she thinks what she thinks. Knowing this, she communicates to students a confidence-inducing sense of being grounded. This sense of groundedness stabilizes her when she feels swept along by forces she cannot control. (p. 23)

I am more comfortable seeking out the thoughts and advice of colleagues (and students) now, knowing that there are always ideas and perspectives that I haven't thought of. I used to think taking time out from my day-to-day work to reflect on my practice was a luxury; now I know it is a necessity.

Small Group Work

A group is a wonderful learning ground. Sharron says, "I could never learn on my own what I have in this group." That seemed to be true for all of the women in the writing group. It was certainly true for me. Working with a group of students can present as many challenges as there are people, and then some. The day-to-day dynamics of group work can be unpredictable. Being involved in a group, as in a family, can be exhausting one day and exhilarating the next.

Information about running and managing small groups for literacy instruction is not plentiful. Yet, in my experience, knowing about how a group forms and evolves is key to the success of a participatory approach to learning. It would be extremely valuable for literacy practitioners to have access to professional development that focused specifically on group dynamics and group process in relation to their literacy work.

Group Guidelines

Something we did in the Chapters Program that I wish we had done in the Women's Writing Group was to create a set of guidelines within which to operate. In the Chapters Program, the women wrote the guidelines themselves.

> ### The Chapters Commitment
>
> Each woman agrees to do her best to
>
> ◇ respect the uniqueness and ability of each person in the program
>
> ◇ be fair and helpful with comments
>
> ◇ help create an accepting place to learn
>
> ◇ pass on activities she doesn't want to take part in
>
> ◇ respect the confidentiality of the people in the program
>
> ◇ give everyone an equal opportunity to speak
>
> ◇ be a good listener
>
> ◇ give everyone the right to her own opinion
>
> ◇ express her needs for quiet time or time out
>
> ◇ contact coordinator or class member if she was unable to attend
>
> ◇ play an active part in building and shaping the program.

Guidelines help group members feel safe and valued. They also act as a starting point as well as a place to come back to if the group has trouble functioning effectively. There was one point in the Women's Writing Group when three out of the six women involved brought their babies with them to the classroom. We all found this very disruptive and were at a loss for how to handle the situation. Once we brought the issue into the open, we were able to find a solution in having the children cared for by students in an Early Childhood Development Program at our local college. The women decided as a group that it was better (for everyone) not to have babies in the classroom. This could have been one of our guidelines.

What It Means to Participate—Setting Expectations

Different people participate in families, in life and in learning settings in different ways. There is no single right way to participate in a learning setting. For example, as literacy workers, it is important to recognize that it is not our failing if a student doesn't show leadership within a group by learning to chair a meeting. Attending the meeting and staying present may be all a student is able to do at that time. That is enough. We need to be careful and conscious about our expectations. There is a difference between expecting people to participate fully where we set the learning agenda and to fully participate, understanding that the students will help to set the agenda and create the learning outcomes. I agree with Campbell (1996) when she says

> Perhaps literacy workers and students may be more accepting of perceived failures if they view participatory literacy practices as a process that gradually evolves over time rather than as a product such as serving on the board or forming a student group. This means we need to challenge the production-oriented discourse which shapes our practice. We need to set aside time to discuss issues such as (a) "What does participatory practices mean?" (b) "What threatens and excites us?" and (c) "What are the benefits and barriers of participatory practice?" (p. 140)

If I had known more about participatory practices when I began working with the Women's Writing Group, we might have been able to discuss and set more reasonable expectations for ourselves. Discussion about participatory practices before and during the learning process are invaluable, especially if this is new ground for everyone. The women in the group were forthcoming with their thoughts in our discussions; however, I should have been more prepared and specific with questions that made sure the women were participating in a way they needed and wanted to, not just in the way that I needed and wanted them to.

Patience with Process

Early in my reading about participatory approaches, I came across an article by Cranton (1996) about the role of the educator in participatory education that I found very intimidating.

> The role of the educator in transformative (participatory) group learning varies over time. The educator begins the process by giving up position power (formal authority and control) but maintaining and using personal power (expertise, authenticity, and loyalty). Equal participation in discourse is encouraged and learner decision making is promoted. This sets the stage for critical self-reflection. When an atmosphere of comfort and collaboration is established, the educator's role becomes one of stimulating reflection through critical questioning and consciousness-raising activities such as role playing, simulations and journal writing. Using experiential techniques and critical incidents can also be helpful. It is

essential that the educator not impose his or her own perspectives on learners but rather encourage individuals to question their own perspectives. Equally important to challenging learners is the provision of support. Questioning one's assumptions can be disconcerting or even painful. The educator should remain authentic and trustworthy, foster group members' support of each other, and encourage networks both within and outside of the group itself. Conflict must be handled with care, and support must be available for personal adjustments and/or those individuals who choose to act on changes they make as a result of the group's work. (p. 31)

Cranton doesn't mention, however, how long all this will take. In reality, promoting and establishing a more participatory program takes time, commitment, knowledge and a great deal of patience. There is also no mention of the variables that can affect the dynamics, progress and readiness of the group. There were many factors that influenced us in the Women's Writing Group. Some influences were obvious (personal health), others more insidious (need for trust and comfort). Some were external (weather), others internal (group dynamics). Because variables are unpredictable, it needs to be recognized that introducing a more participatory approach into a learning setting takes time, understanding and patience on everyone's part. The group (including the facilitator) needs to work as a team, sharing the same goals, setbacks and expectations.

Not for Everyone

When I first started to read about using a more participatory approach in adult literacy education, I was very excited about it. I felt good about the level of participation students had demonstrated in the Chapters Program and looked forward to being able to offer an opportunity for women to increase that level of participation in the writing group. I learned that even though a participatory approach sounded appealing, it wasn't necessarily what the students wanted, or what they were comfortable with. And I have to admit, even though I still believe in the philosophy of participatory education, I'm not sure it's what I wanted or was comfortable with either.

I know now that a participatory approach to learning is not a cut-and-dried technique. The interest of the students in being more active in their own learning can vary from day to day and from student to student, requiring the teacher to be incredibly flexible with her ability to step in or step back. She may, in fact, have to be a facilitator/encourager with one student and an instructor with another, all at the same time, all in the same room! I have also learned that involving students more in their learning and the learning that is happening around them takes a certain readiness on everyone's part. It cannot be forced, only suggested and encouraged. As instructors, we have to model the approach while still building trust and credibility. I do think it's worth the effort, but it can sometimes be exhausting, hard work. (my journal)

I assumed a lot when we started the Women's Writing Group. I assumed that it was in the students' best interest to be more involved in their learning. I thought it would be good for them to learn to facilitate a group. I assumed they thought so, too. But once the group got going, it was clear that not everyone wanted to take on a leadership role as prominent as facilitating the group. Some were happy with making the coffee and making sure everyone had pens and paper. One woman found being in front of the group so frightening she took a tranquilizer before her turn to speak.

I will always look at the work I do now with an eye for possibilities for students to participate. However, a fully participatory program is not for everyone. Each person involved in a program has her own individual needs and abilities to consider. Some facets of a more participatory approach, however, might be very appropriate for a student (or the instructor). Sharron wrote one day:

> *I could never go back to the old style of learning where the teacher is in the front of the room and all the students sit in rows. Before all the "goodie goodies" sat in the front and all the brats at the back. Here we're all mixed up together and I like that way better!*

I will remember how important it is to think through and reflect with a student on each step she takes towards greater independence and leadership. Is this truly what she wants? Is she ready to stand in front of an audience with a microphone in front of her? Is she saying she is ready because she wants to please me, or because she truly is ready? Maybe if I had asked more of those questions I might have been better able to let go when I needed to, and been more understanding when people resisted the involvement they originally said they wanted.

A Year Later

the Bad News . . .

The doors of the LeapFrog Women's Co-operative closed 15 months after they opened. Three weeks later, word was received that Canada Alberta Services was willing to fund a skills-for-work program for women at the co-operative. Unfortunately it was too late. After 15 months of community awareness events, fundraising, proposal writing and board meetings, the women involved in the co-operative were tired and disillusioned. Although they had been very committed to the idea of the co-op, after a while they lost sight of the original goals of the co-operative. I think now that the expectations of the group and those who supported them were set unrealistically high. The women involved did not have the necessary (complicated) skills to organize and run a co-operative. Some of the women were so determined to do it themselves that they rejected any offer of leadership or support from experienced community members.

When the women involved in the Women's Writing Group (who were only partially involved in the planning of the co-operative) talk about LeapFrog now, they talk about how the women hadn't worked as a team, how some of the people involved wanted all the control and were not prepared to work with all the members of the steering committee. Some of the people involved weren't ready for the changes and ideas others were promoting. There was little communication. When I look back on it now, I can see that there were a lot of difficult group dynamics happening within the working group that no one was willing or able to recognize, let alone do anything about. One day Alice said, *A frog can't jump backwards, but if he gets turned around, somehow he can end up going back where he came from and not going forward at all.* That's how she summed up what happened to the LeapFrog Women's Co-operative.

. . . and the Good News

After my work with the Women's Writing Group came to an end, I began work on the Write to Learn Project[2], which is designed to promote the value and use of writing in literacy programming. Part of the project has been to provide what we call "fearless writing" workshops to literacy program students and instructors in different communities across Canada. Sharron, Alice and Barb, who were part

[2]The Write to Learn Project is a three year project (1998–2001) funded by the National Literacy Secretariat, Human Resources Development Canada.

of the Women's Writing Group, are now working with me in the Write to Learn Project as writing ambassadors[3]. They speak comfortably in public about how they used to be uncomfortable with writing and how writing has helped them in their lives. They have facilitated writing workshops for students and instructors in literacy programs from Yellowknife, NWT, to St. John's, NF. Two of the women traveled to Ottawa as invited presenters at a national conference on literacy and health. They facilitated a workshop where participants wrote about health issues. Their start in Chapters and the Women's Writing Group gave them the interest and confidence to continue learning about participating more in a group. There are still many factors that influence their participation, but we are more aware of them and able to work with these factors more effectively.

The Write to Learn Project has been hugely successful, which wouldn't have been possible without Sharron, Barb and Alice's brave and generous participation.

A Final Thought

As I finished up the work on this research paper, it suddenly occurred to me that I had learned more about changing roles than I realized. I hadn't seen myself as a researcher before, but over the past year I had actually become one! And I also realized that I had struggled with that new role in ways similar to how the women in the writing group and I struggled with the changes in our roles within the group.

Just as the women had felt unsure about being facilitators, I had thought I wasn't smart enough to be a researcher. I was scared of failing or seeming inadequate but I was also intrigued by the challenge. I didn't want anyone to know how difficult I found all this thinking to be. When the other members of the Research in Practice Project got together, I was afraid to speak because I didn't think my comments were intelligent or academic enough. People said to me, "Don't be silly; of course you can do it," which of course meant nothing to me until I could believe it myself.

There are so many parallels in my own story to the women's hesitation to take on the role of facilitator in the writing group. Perhaps it is just human nature to be afraid to leave the comfort of what we know, to venture out and try something new. This project and my own struggles have taught me never to underestimate the

[3]Sharron, Alice and Barb also wrote *Fearless freewriting*. (2000). Edmonton, AB. Voices Rising/Learning at the Centre Press.

importance of personal readiness, or the value of asking for and accepting help and encouragement as we continue to grow and learn. I learned from the women in the writing group that not everyone wants to play the role of facilitator. They did say, however, that they were glad to have had the opportunity to learn about what it means to facilitate a group. And I'm glad that I had the opportunity to learn about research and the research process. Maybe I won't choose to continue doing research, but at least now I know what it is all about. It feels good to know, through the work I did on this project, that I can now make that choice.

References

Brookfield, S. (1995). *What it means to be a critically reflective teacher.* San Francisco: Jossey-Bass.

Campbell, P. (1996). Participatory literacy practices: Exploring social identity and relations. *Adult Basic Education, 6*(3), 127-142.

Cranton, P. (1996). Types of group learning. *New Directions for Adult and Continuing Education, 71*, 25-32.

Hayes, E., & Walter, P. G. (1995). A comparison of small group learning approaches in adult literacy education. *Adult Basic Education, 5*(3), 133-151.

Hughes, E. F. (1992). *Writing from the inner self.* New York: Harper Collins.

Morgan, D. M. (1997). *Writing out loud.* Camrose, AB: Morgan Consulting Services.

Sharron, Barb & Alice. (2000). *Fearless freewriting.* Edmonton, AB: Voices Rising/Learning at the Centre Press.

YWCA of Metropolitan Toronto. (1982). *The dynamics of life skills.* Saskatchewan NewStart Inc., Training Research and Development Station.

Chapter 7

First Steps in Participatory Practice

Linda Keam

Linda Keam

First Steps in Participatory Practice

Program Context

I work as the Coordinator/Instructor of the Literacy and Academic Upgrading Programs for the John Howard Society (JHS) in a large urban centre. Our learners are men, women and youth who have been involved or might be at risk of involvement with the criminal justice system. The family members of our learners are also able to access the literacy and upgrading programs.

The majority of our learners are involved in the adult literacy program, receiving one-to-one assistance from a volunteer tutor. While most learners live in the community, including some at our halfway house, several are in the Young Offender Centre, and others are incarcerated in one of three other local correctional institutions. A small number of learners pursue their academic upgrading through attendance at the JHS Learning Opportunities Centre, where they work on individualized programs with instructor support.

Recent graduate research (Selme, 1998) that I carried out on the literacy education of federally incarcerated women made me aware that prison education programs in Alberta and Saskatchewan at the basic literacy and upgrading levels offer little, if any, opportunity for significant intellectual growth or the development of critical thinking skills. Historically prison education in Canada has come under heavy criticism. According to Cosman (1981):

> Penitentiary education in Canada has been characterized by a general lack of interest in genuine educational achievement, by a lack of discrimination in matters of curriculum between the trivial and the important . . . lack of discipline and structure, and by a complete lack of educational research. (p. 40)

Incarcerated women and men function in an environment in which they tend to be infantilized, and where they are for the most part deprived of any personal power or opportunities for decision-making. To counter this tendency, the JHS literacy and upgrading programs offer learners the opportunity and encouragement necessary to take an active role in framing their individual learning experiences, with the assistance and encouragement of their tutor or instructor.

Historically, however, learners in our programs have not been offered opportunities to participate in program or project planning. Each year proposals must be submitted by the coordinator to potential funders to ensure the continuation of the literacy and upgrading programs, and decisions are made and programs planned according to funders' criteria months in advance of program commencement. From that point the coordinator maintains sole control of the projects.

Tutors are encouraged to work closely with their learners in acquiring appropriate curricular materials, but learners have not been afforded the opportunity to work together to contribute to the development of curricular activities which would draw on their interests, knowledge, skills and expertise.

While development of reading and writing skills is fundamental to a literacy program, Jurmo (1989) contends such skill development is an inadequate literacy program goal:

> Literacy programs need to be structured to enhance the development of additional characteristics, including critical thinking or problem-solving, ability to work collaboratively with others, self-esteem, and interest in continuing one's education. (p. 20)

These personal qualities are deemed basic to the development of a healthy, mature adult, and without such qualities, a learner is "likely to remain passive and not even use the technical skills that he or she already has" (Jurmo, 1989, pp. 20-21).

In September 1997, our local John Howard Society received project funding from the National Literacy Secretariat to address the need for high interest, appropriate and relevant literacy learning materials for youth in conflict with the law, and to give youth the opportunity to take an active rather than passive role in the development of learning materials for use by themselves and their peers, and in their own literacy learning and continuing educational endeavours.

Our JHS Participatory Curriculum Development Project held as its objectives:

- to develop learning materials/curricula intended for the specific population of young men and women currently or formerly incarcerated or involved with the criminal justice system

- to facilitate learner participation in curriculum creation

- to make available to learners and teachers in both provincial and federal correctional institutions within Alberta the resultant curriculum document

- to encourage and promote ongoing participatory literacy activities with offenders and ex-offenders, within and outside of prison school settings, with the curriculum document and the curriculum creation process potentially serving as model and catalyst for both learners and teachers

The participatory nature of this project made it an ideal focus for my involvement in the Participatory Approaches/Research in Practice Project reported in this chapter.

Research Question

While struggling to define my research question, I wondered if our learners would actually be interested in or have the time and energy for taking part in such a participatory project, given their need to deal with so many crucial life issues. Would they want to be part of a project which would present academic challenges outside of their experience? And most importantly, would their involvement prove personally beneficial to them? Therefore my research question became:

> When learners are given the opportunity to participate in a curriculum development project, what form will that participation take, and how will learners benefit from such participation?

Inviting Participant Involvement

Historically the JHS Literacy and Upgrading Programs have been offered through one-to-one tutoring or independent study with instructor assistance, both for learners in the community and for those residing in correctional institutions. As it is quite unusual for any two learners to be working on the same subject or at the same level at any given time, and as it is often difficult for learners to gather at one single location because of the size of the city, the costs and time involved in travelling by public transit, and in some cases employment schedules, it has been difficult to incorporate group work into learning opportunities offered in a program. It was therefore very challenging to assemble a group of learners willing to participate in this project.

Letters of invitation were sent to all learners in the JHS Literacy and Upgrading programs, inviting their participation in the curriculum development project, and inviting their submissions of stories and poems for inclusion in the booklet. A letter was also sent to each of the tutors advising them of the project and encouraging them to work with their learners on writings for the booklet, with the hope they would also encourage their learners to participate in the project. In addition, I invited learners demonstrating a commitment to academic upgrading in the Learning Opportunities Centre to take part in the project. While no response was received from our Literacy learners, four of the five Learning Opportunities Centre learners accepted: Fred, Nilda, Breeann and Jackie.

An explanation of the project was given to each participant and then participants were asked individually to sit on a committee for the project. When a person agreed to take part in the project, a formal consent form (modelled after those required by the local university for research with human subjects) was presented and read to him or her prior to signing. All participants wished to have their real first names used in any reporting of the project.

The project was defined, planned and in place many months prior to the participants' involvement. Participation in the project was planned to, and did, take the following forms:

- As a committee they would choose the poems/stories to be included in the booklet.

- Prior to deciding which submissions would be accepted, committee members would create a list of criteria upon which to base their decisions.

- The committee would choose the layout for the booklet, the order in which the writings would appear, and learner artwork that was suitable for enhancing the appeal of the booklet.

- The committee would create some of the curricular activities to be included in the booklet. (I believed the creation of activities to accompany the writings in the booklet would be a fairly difficult task. I did not expect the participants to come up with all the activities which would be required to make the final document a solid and worthwhile resource, but did expect committee members would bring forward ideas for suitable activities which other literacy learners would find meaningful and worthwhile.)

- The committee would plan and host the World Literacy Day celebration at which the booklet would be launched.

As well, committee members were asked to participate in my research about the project through writing and interviews, as described below.

Collection and Analysis of Data

I collected data in the following ways during the course of the project.

- I made notes and/or tape-recorded the meetings I deemed most critical to the project.

- I asked committee members to write about their experiences (thoughts and feelings) of being involved in the project, both at a point early in their involvement, and again later following the World Literacy Day celebration and booklet launch.

- To ensure input from a third party source, I contracted a professor from the local university's Faculty of Education to act as project consultant. She conducted semi-structured interviews with project participants and attended the most significant meetings of the committee. Semi-structured interviews were chosen to encourage participant input beyond the interview questions I had developed.

- I kept fieldnotes on my observations of the learners as they worked on the project together outside of formal committee meetings.

- I kept a reflective journal in which I documented and explored my thoughts and feelings about the research project.

The data were analysed in the following ways.

- Meeting transcripts were analysed for level and type of learner input and participation.

- Fieldnotes were examined for evidence of participant involvement in the project.

- Interview transcripts were examined for self-reported perceptions of involvement in the project and for indications of personal benefits received.

- Participants' writings were analysed for themes which directly addressed the research question. I also sought to determine if similar ideas and/or areas of concern were reflected in more than one participant's writings.

- My reflective journal was analysed for themes arising from my experience of the project. I chose as themes those ideas and strands of thinking which recurred throughout the life of the project, determining their significance by the frequency with which they were written about and the impact they had on my participation in the project.

Forms of Participation
Group Work

Though it took several months, a group of four learners was formed to take part in this project with me. The first learner, Fred, assumed a leadership role from the beginning (March), coming to the first formal meeting with a prepared, typed agenda. He maintained this leadership role for the duration of the project. He seemed not entirely happy when Nilda joined the committee in April, but this was short-lived, and within a short time the two of them were working well together. As Breeann and Jackie joined the committee (August), such resistance to sharing the project did not seem to recur. Fred and Nilda were quite welcoming when Jackie and Breeann joined the group.

As the first two participants involved, Fred and Nilda spent a considerable amount of time working together on the project:

> *We even took time ourselves when Linda wasn't around to discuss, well, we've got to do this, we've got to do that, and what should be done. We seemed to get together on that.* (Fred, interview)

Later Breeann and Jackie worked closely together. Breeann assisted Jackie with some of the more challenging literacy activities. She helped with determining criteria for acceptance of writings for the booklet and creating learning activities to accompany the chosen submissions.

Several months before the booklet was complete and before the World Literacy Day Celebration, Nilda was transferred to the local Remand Centre, from which temporary absences are not granted. She was unable to attend the meetings of the committee, so I met with her in Remand on Thursday mornings, and shared the work of the rest of the committee with her. At our Friday morning committee meetings I shared with the rest of the group the ideas Nilda and I had discussed the previous day. I felt the group continued to work cohesively, in spite of Nilda's absence from the committee meetings, but Fred found this way of working difficult. During his interview he stated:

I figure the biggest point is discussion, and we lost that when she [Nilda] was incarcerated. I had to go through Linda to talk, and if I had anything Linda took it to her, and we went that way. . . . That was a drawback for me. . . . I found that a little frustrating.

Although we attempted to hold committee meetings every week, learner participants' changing work schedules, appointments, crises and incarceration made it difficult to get everyone together at the same time.

By mid-August, the committee members were working diligently to finalize their criteria for inclusion of writings in the booklet. As World Literacy Day rapidly approached, we realized it would be impossible to include the learning activities in the booklet to be launched at the World Literacy Day celebration. I decided the committee could continue with the learning activities segment of the booklet after the celebration. We revised our objectives. The committee determined the criteria for inclusion; read, discussed and decided which writings should be included; and then turned their attention toward planning the celebration in great detail, from the food and decorations to the guest list and activities.

Following a very successful World Literacy Day celebration, the committee began the challenging work of creating learning activities to correspond with the writings chosen for the booklet. Notwithstanding Nilda's continuing incarceration, all members of the committee contributed learning activities for the booklet. Once their involvement in the project came to an end in November, the committee was dissolved.

Expanding the Parameters

At the beginning of the project, I was very clear about how it would unfold. Literacy and Upgrading Program learners would submit their writings and art work for the booklet and our committee would 1) draw up criteria for inclusion, 2) read and discuss each piece in order to make our decisions, and 3) create curricular/learning activities to correspond with each text. The booklet would be typed up and printed, and on World Literacy Day we'd celebrate with the launch of the booklet and some great food.

However, I had underestimated the committee members. With their shared focus on the booklet, they met together spontaneously in the Learning Centre to work on the project between regularly-scheduled committee meetings, and came up with ideas for the project which I had neither included nor planned to include.

Nilda decided that because so few people knew who John Howard was, a short biography on him should be included in the booklet, and she undertook research at the city's main library to write a suitable piece. Incarcerated in a local minimum-security institution and attending the JHS Learning Centre under daily temporary absences, Nilda advocated for the project to other inmates by inviting them to submit writings for the booklet. Upon being sent back to the Remand Centre, from which temporary absences were not allowed, she spoke with the correctional officers of her participation in the project. This resulted in two officers requesting an invitation to the World Literacy Day event.

Fred approached participants and staff of the Youth in Care and Custody Network (which maintains an office in our building) and later his peers in the JHS Employment Program for writings for the booklet. He also urged me to contact inmates in all the local correctional facilities and invite their submissions. As a result of Jackie reading her poems aloud during one of the committee meetings, the parameters of the project were further stretched to include the possibility of tape-recording the authors reading their writings to accompany the booklet.

Infusing Energy

Like most Literacy Coordinators, I am used to working in relative isolation. Thus I was surprised and delighted at the amount of energy the other participants brought to the project and to me.

> I don't have to work in isolation; others are dynamically involved, offering ideas, insights, and sharing the workload. The enthusiasm the learners demonstrate is particularly heartwarming. Their degree of involvement and their desire to be more involved is a very pleasant surprise. (reflective journal)

Sharing Power in the Group

The committee members were engaged in many literacy activities themselves. They drew up criteria for including writings in the booklet. Some of the writings they selected were their own. They went on to create corresponding activities to go with the writings. In addition to the reading and writing they did for the booklet project, they were also asked to write about the experience of being involved in the project. They focused on two points in the project: shortly after they joined the committee and then following the World Literacy Day celebration.

One meeting was spent discussing the criteria for inclusion. Fred had drawn up a list of ten criteria which he presented to the committee. None of the others offered additional ideas for criteria. As Fred's submission proved very appropriate, his criteria were confirmed as the ones to guide the selection of the writings.

Once the criteria had been set, participants were given copies of the writings submitted. They were asked to read them and choose writings for inclusion in the booklet. Fred's suggestion that committee members put in writing their reasons for choosing or excluding each piece of writing was accepted by the committee, and each participant did so.

At the following meeting, committee members discussed each piece of writing and made decisions about inclusion. In light of the criteria, Nilda had some difficulty with a story in which the author used the phrase "bust your ass." After discussion about whether or not the phrase would be offensive to others and whether the author should be asked to rephrase his idea, the committee chose to include the story as it had been written.

In discussing a poem they felt was problematic in rhythm, one committee member suggested we remove a line in order to make the poem work. Following a short period of silence Jackie asked, "Can we do that?" Her question lead to a discussion of "editorial ethics," and it was decided to return the poem to the author with a request for revision. The committee created several alternatives for the author to consider in her reworking of the piece.

In mid-November a meeting was held to work on learning activities. (Prior to this I had done brainstorming sessions with Jackie because she was experiencing a great deal of anxiety around this task.) Each participant offered wonderful ideas for activities that other literacy learners would find interesting. For example, Breeann suggested that several blank lined pages be included in the booklet for literacy learners to fill with their stories and poems. She felt this opportunity for personal work would complete the booklet.

One idea the committee had about the order in which the writings would appear was to have the poems at the beginning with the stories following (in essence, items ordered by length). However, after reflection they decided the writings should be grouped in order of subject matter or theme.

Thus while the learner participants may not have realized it, in making editorial decisions, they engaged in some fairly sophisticated literacy activities, at a level far beyond what I had anticipated.

Sharing of Gifts

Beyond the tasks entailed in the compilation of the booklet, the participants brought many personal gifts and talents to the project. They demonstrated kindness and compassion towards each other as they struggled with some of the more difficult literacy aspects of the project. They offered their enthusiasm for the project and brought a high level of energy to it.

At the World Literacy Day celebration they shared their culinary and artistic gifts and talents; they welcomed their guests warmly and attended to their needs. They shared their thoughts and feelings about the booklet and the project with the guests, which included family members and friends. And to the overall project they brought great fun and laughter, and an infusion of creative ideas which greatly enriched the project and everyone's participation in it.

Barriers/Limitations to Learner Participation

The original project had been developed well in advance of active learner participation, thus the learners had no input into overall design and focus. Although participants expressed an interest and desire to be more involved, there were barriers to their doing so. While I had hoped to have the committee work together to write the letter of invitation for the World Literacy Day celebration, it was impossible to get everyone together during the critical time in which the invitations needed to be sent. Due to confidentiality concerns, I was unable to have participants address the envelopes to program learners and tutors, even though one participant in particular had expressed the desire to do more. She had also offered to transcribe the tapes of one of the significant meetings, which she had been unable to attend. Due to the lengthy process involved in transcribing audiotapes, and my desire to have the transcription done at the earliest possible time, I chose to complete the task myself. In the interview done by the project consultant with this participant, it became apparent she was also interested in working on the writing of this report, but felt she did not have the education required to do so. I had not anticipated the participants would be interested in engaging in these kinds of activities. My view of the contributions learners could or would make was more limited than experience subsequently attested. I underestimated the learners in many ways.

On the other hand, I may have overestimated them in other ways. Some participants may have found the expectations of the project (choosing and editing pieces of writing for inclusion in the booklet, setting criteria for inclusion) to be difficult, which caused them undue anxiety. I took a great deal for granted. For instance, I asked the participants to come up with "criteria" for the pieces of writing to be accepted. I was concerned that some participants might not understand what was meant by the word, although I did try to define it for them in several ways; i.e., what would be acceptable as content, subject matter, and use of language. How would we know if a piece of writing was good or suitable for other literacy learners at various levels of ability? However, the language I used may have proven exclusionary.

I was therefore quite surprised by the energy and enthusiasm with which they participated on the project. Although they were asked to undertake academic tasks to which they may have felt inadequate, nonetheless they put a fair amount of work into them.

Fred voiced his preference for working in a group as opposed to working alone. Fred and Nilda spend a lot of time discussing their ideas for the project with each other, as did Breeann and Jackie. Although I felt group participation remained adequate and intact even after Nilda was incarcerated with no temporary absence privileges, Fred found it difficult without the face-to-face discussion. He said, *It was so hard to discover her thoughts from reading little sets of ideas . . . from her . . . to realize what she really meant by it.*

Benefits of Participation for Learners

It was my sincere hope the learner-participants would enjoy being involved in the project with each other and with me. I hoped they would have the opportunity to learn and grow, both academically and personally, while they engaged in the many activities associated with the project. Each acknowledged enjoyment in participation, which suggests my hopes were in some measure realized.

As an educator, I perceived further benefits: that their potential contribution to future literacy learners and tutors, teachers in correctional centres, and others who will use the booklet's writings and activities as a vehicle to help increase literacy skills is significant; that they benefited from the development of fairly complex literacy, problem-solving and critical thinking skills; that the supportive group atmosphere which they developed and maintained throughout the project will continue to benefit them; and that they were proud of their own achievements at the World Literacy Day celebration, surrounded by family and friends. Each learner-participant was dealing with some fairly serious life-issues during the life of the project. I believe their project work allowed them freedom from the usual course of their days. It gave them something else to think about, beyond their meeting with parole or probation officers and lawyers, returning to the correctional institution in the evenings, and the like. I observed their delight upon seeing the completed booklet (version one), which included some of their own writings and their names in the front acknowledging their involvement in the booklet's creation. I identified these benefits; two participants identified some of their own. In her interview, Jackie stated:

> I think the best part for me was me being able to go home and write some poems, and at the same time not knowing if they'd be part of the project. And in the end they were accepted and nobody even found no mistakes in my poems. So being involved and having accomplished something and seeing it on paper.

> I'm so used to not having to learn, or say or do anything. That was my first time being out doing and being in that kind of class. So therefore, it got me to open up and to express my thoughts, where I usually keep them to myself, so Linda had me talking and stuff, expressing my views, so I think I really opened up. The first meeting I really didn't have too much to say, but a couple of meetings later I started opening my mouth, and it got easier and easier, so I started enjoying it.

> I understand literacy better now than I ever have, cause I always thought that I was pretty illiterate. And I know now that I'm not. But a literacy program can help the slower people, and I am a slower people, so it helped me have a different look, a lot more confidence.

Breeann indicated a benefit in the area of literacy as well. Some of the poems that were submitted for inclusion in the booklet contained words with which she wasn't familiar, which led her to conclude:

> I need to educate myself more on words or stuff so I can understand, 'cause there are some poems that came in with words I didn't understand. I want to know more about the English language. I tried to be more intellectual about [my reading and

writing], I guess. I think that's the word I'm trying to use. This project made me think of different words I could use. Like I would look in a synonym book, and what words would go, instead of "that was great." Everything was "great." So what other words would go? That's what it made me do. That was kind of neat. . . . Instead of "That was good," like those words are so plain. You could have words like "intriguing." Things like that sound better, I think.

It's a good learning process for a person, I think, this type of group. Because it makes you know yourself better, because you're looking into somebody else's stuff, and then you see what you could do to correct yourself. Like, I didn't like this poem or this sentence because of this reason. Well, what about me? If I was writing a poem, what kind of understandings would I want people to understand through my poem? So that's what I try to do, and I think its important for people to know those things. It gets you to check yourself as well.

Breeann felt she had the opportunity to make important decisions about the project, particularly in helping to choose which poems and stories would be included in the booklet.

It made me feel important, and it was important because I'm choosing . . . helping people decide whether or not this person's poem should go in or not. And there's a lot of thought to that, because they all have different characteristics and stuff.

During the interview, none of Fred's comments touched on self-identified positive benefits from his involvement in the program. Rather, there were several areas of concern, some of which are reflected elsewhere in this report.

It was not possible to interview Nilda, as she had been transferred to a correctional centre several hundred miles away and was subsequently deported.

Reflections on My Participation

What an incredible learning experience this project has been for me! Inner struggles regarding the sharing of power and control were frequent. Throughout the life of the project, constraints on time proved an unwelcome and constant challenge: time for reflective writing and deep thought about the project, and for writing the research report, was especially affected.

Because time was short, I experienced periods of intense frustration when the committee members expanded the parameters of the project by including components beyond those originally conceived. It was often difficult to be true to the participatory nature of the project rather than taking control over every facet. However, I found it easy to completely give over planning the World Literacy Day celebration and booklet launch, undoubtedly because it was non-academic in nature.

It was difficult, too, to find a balance between being in charge of this project for which I held responsibility to the funder, and at the other end being a noncontributing observer. I struggled constantly to be one with the other members of the committee, but found it difficult to gain and maintain such balance.

Yet neither had I anticipated the many positive benefits of working with a group on a project such as this. The participants brought new ideas, heightened the energy levels around the project, and offered their gifts. I didn't have to work in isolation, because others were dynamically involved. When given the opportunity to participate, the learners jumped at the chance and they far exceeded my limited expectations of them. Although the project placed the participants in a setting quite different from their day-to-day environments, and while what was being asked of them was in some ways quite complex, I was quite surprised by some of the literacy work they were doing. Through the surprise I experienced when the participants offered some astounding, insightful comments, I realized I had cast these four people in a deficit role. My assumptions regarding their abilities were significantly challenged.

I saw myself reflected in these learners as well. I experienced a great deal of stress around the reporting of this project. I had just completed a Master's Degree, barely completed the thesis defense, and here I was again writing a research report. Once again I was feeling inadequate to the task before me. Were the project facilitators expecting things from me I couldn't deliver? Although I frequently reminded myself that this was a research report, not a thesis, I wondered if they would be expecting the type of rich data that researchers pray for. Because I so greatly admired the abilities and work of one of my fellow-researchers in this larger project, I agonized over every thought, every word, in order to not prove an embarrassment to the project and not embarrass myself in front of my peers. I endeavoured to find a voice that better expressed my delight in having the learners involved in the project with me, yet I remained trapped in the formal academic language I had learned so well. While I've never needed to be at the top of the class, I've always worked diligently to avoid looking stupid. Much like Jackie, who sought out Breeann to give her the "right" answers, and who felt inadequate to her task, I spent an inordinate amount of time (unfortunately for the most part in solitude) searching for the right answers, the right ideas, the perfect quotations, to include in this report. I hesitated to seek assistance from the project coordinator or the research facilitator because I didn't want to appear inadequate to *my* task. Thus, I seemed to have cast myself in the same deficit role as I cast the learner-participants.

Much time has passed since the four committee members worked with me on this project. My hope had been for each to experience a boost in self-esteem that would prove life-changing, and in the short-term this hope was probably realized. Long-term evidence of benefit is either unavailable or equivocal. One learner has been deported and is having a difficult time coping with a life in abject poverty. Another participant has experienced a number of crises in recent months. Yet perhaps the project can be perceived as an oasis in the participants' lives, a time and place in which they were able to concentrate their energies and gifts on a project outside their normal experience of life. Perhaps they found respite in a place of safety and acceptance if even for only a brief period in their lives.

References

Cosman, J. W. (1981). Penitentiary education in Canada. In L. Morin (Ed.), *On prison education*. (p. 34) Ottawa: Canadian Government Publishing Centre.

Jurmo, P. (1989). The case for participatory literacy education. *New Directions for Continuing Education, 42,* 17-34.

Selme, L. (1998). *The Literacy education of federally incarcerated women*. Unpublished master's thesis. University of Calgary, Calgary, AB.

Chapter 8

Challenges to Sharing Power in an Adult Literacy Education Program

Mary Norton

Mary Norton

Challenges to Sharing Power in an Adult Literacy Education Program

Introduction

Sharing power among teachers and learners is a basic principle of participatory education. When some students at The Learning Centre decided to host a student conference, I had an opportunity to research whether and how I practise this principle. During six months, I worked with students to plan, organize, host and celebrate a successful event. With students' permission, I documented our work, and used these documents to learn about sharing power. What follows is an account of my learning.

Context

The Learning Centre is an adult literacy and education centre at the Boyle Street Co-op, a community resources and services agency on the edge of downtown Edmonton. The Centre was started in 1981 to provide one-to-one tutoring and learning support for adults in Edmonton's inner-city neighbourhoods. Today, women and men come to the Centre from nearby neighbourhoods and farther afield to learn and to teach, to engage in meaningful activity, and to be with others. I have been involved with the Centre since 1981 for similar reasons: as a government consultant to literacy programs, as a volunteer, and, since 1992, as a paid program coordinator and learning facilitator.

I was attracted to The Learning Centre because it offered possibilities to engage in participatory education. According to Jurmo (1989), participatory education means that students have "higher degrees of control, responsibility and reward vis-à-vis program activities" (p. 17). Gaber-Katz and Watson (1991) suggest that student participation includes a range of activities, from learner-centred lesson development to becoming active in the community.

Auerbach (1993) distinguishes between participatory education and other participatory approaches by recalling participatory education's origins in popular education. As well as encouraging active student participation, popular education engages people in analysing power relations and organizing action to change oppressive conditions. (Arnold, Barndt and Burke, 1985; Merrifield, 1999; Ross, 1997).

In the 1970s I had been introduced to popular education and related perspectives about education for social change. I explored those perspectives during the 1980s, mainly through reading, research, writing and discussion. I embraced a critical perspective about literacy education and connections between low literacy, poverty and how power is distributed in society. Since 1992, I have been able to test those perspectives in daily practice and through a series of participatory projects. Like others, I have come to believe that literacy programs can provide opportunities for people to experience more equitable power relationships—at least within programs—and to gain skills and confidence to participate more equally in other settings (Auerbach, 1993; Campbell, 1996; Jurmo, 1989).

In my first year as a coordinator with the Centre, I explored ways to invite students into participatory activities. In 1993, following a visioning process with students and volunteers, the Centre moved into a larger space and began to accommodate group learning. There were areas where people could work together, as well as spaces to work alone or with a tutor. While one-to-one tutoring remained an option for students, many chose to learn in groups as well.

Starting in 1994, a peer tutoring project involved a number of students in tutoring other students. Research about the project found that peer tutoring enhanced learning, nurtured growth of confidence and self-esteem, and enabled the development of personal relationships among students. As well, peer tutoring "invited a shift in social/power relations among students, tutors and staff . . ." (Norton, 1996, p.7). As facilitator for the project, I reflected on what it means to share power with students and found contradictions between my practices and beliefs. This realization, along with continuing reflection on practice, prompted the focus for my research with the conference committee.

Students Meeting Students

In the autumn of 1997, Andrea Pheasey and I became involved in the Participatory Approaches in Adult Literacy Education/Research in Practice Project[1]. We introduced the idea of participatory projects, and students identified a number of ways they participated at the Centre (see Appendix A). In January 1998, Andrea and I organized a meeting for anyone interested in undertaking a specific participatory project. Students brainstormed a number of ideas, including a student

[1]Andrea is a facilitator at The Learning Centre. Her research is reported in Chapter 4.

conference and a computer project. At a follow-up meeting, the list of ideas was narrowed to these two, and people decided which project they wanted to join. Seven students and I opted for the conference project and began to meet once a week, calling ourselves the conference committee. Eventually, the committee included nine students, as three others joined and one left.

Most of us on the committee had some experience with literacy conferences. Helen, Mary, Lil, Tammy and Linda had all attended provincial literacy conferences. Mary and Lil had helped with conference registration tasks. I had been attending and presenting at conferences since the 1970s and had chaired or served on various conference planning groups.

Most committee members also had experiences with participatory approaches. Helen and Mary had served on The Learning Centre board, Lil was currently serving and Helen was a student representative with a provincial literacy organization. Helen, Mary, Barb and Holly had been in the peer tutoring project and all three, along with Lil and Tammy, continued to tutor or be tutored by peers. Four of the women had been in the women's health group, a participatory education project. All of the committee members and I had worked together before, either through one or more of the participatory projects or in one of the learning groups I facilitated.

The conference committee met at least once a week from January to May. After late February, one of the students, Helen, chaired the meetings. As a group the committee decided on purposes and a title for the conference, when and where to hold it and whom to invite.

Students Meeting Students

When: May 29–30, 1998
Where: The Bennett Centre
         9703–94 Street, Edmonton
Who for: • students in literacy programs
         • staff or tutors who want to learn with
           students
What: • meet students from different programs
         • share ideas about student participation
         • go to workshops
         • relax and have fun!

Each committee member took on various tasks before and during the conference. Kathy surveyed students and volunteers at The Learning Centre about interest in attending. Kathy and Linda contacted other literacy programs to invite students. Helen worked on the brochure design and contacted some workshop presenters. Mary and Lil requested and collected items for the registration kits. Lil arranged the entertainment. Helen chaired the conference itself. Mary and Kathy staffed the registration desk and Tammy led an icebreaker activity. Mary, Lil, Linda and Holly facilitated discussion groups.

I filled various roles as I worked with the committee, including facilitator, scribe, coach, tutor, driver and information source. I also managed the budget assigned to the conference project and applied for additional funds for the conference itself.

The committee's work culminated with a residential event at a conference centre in Edmonton's river valley. Thirty-two people, including some tutors and staff, from six literacy programs attended. The beds were too hard but the food was good and the weather was fabulous. People talked, laughed and learned—about themselves, about each other, and about what they could do.

> *We finally got to do something for ourselves, without the staff doing it for us. . . . It feels really good that we can actually do something.* (Holly)

Why do people feel that they can't do things for themselves? If we consider that "power" comes from a root meaning "to be able" (Starhawk, 1987), we can see how feeling able and feeling powerful are linked. As an educator, I want to help students believe that they "can," and I try to help them develop skills so they in fact can. But to what extent do I really help, and how? When do my actions echo other experiences that contributed to students' feeling that they can't? How do I use and misuse my power, as a teacher and a person? These and related questions took form as I worked with the conference committee and undertook my research about sharing power.

Doing the Research

> Research is about asking questions, either of ourselves and/or of others, in order to understand better what's happening around us, and to understand our effects on other people. (Hamilton, 1989, p. 5)

I think about my work a lot. I play back mental tapes and rewrite scripts, hoping to do better next time. My experiences frame my reading about literacy and education, and my reading informs my practices. I may share anxious thoughts with trusted colleagues or use them as examples when I teach other practitioners. However, for me, reflective practice is largely a private process.

Research about my role with the student conference committee was an opportunity to examine my practices systematically. Documenting my work and reviewing documents meant I could look at my practice more carefully and less selectively than with reflective thinking alone. However, with its aim of building and sharing knowledge, research is more public than reflection. Although I welcomed the opportunity to do research about myself in order to improve my practice, writing publicly about myself seems rather self-indulgent. At the same time, I know that my questions and experiences are not unique. In participatory education for change, people are encouraged to share personal experiences—to know we are not alone, to invite analysis, and to plan further action (Arnold, Burke, James, Martin and Thomas, 1991).

Getting Started

As a member of the Participatory Approaches Project, I had access to a research mentor, a role filled by Grace Malicky. I consulted with Grace as I planned, carried out and wrote up my research. Grace also attended some meetings of the conference committee and, at my request, interviewed some of the committee members.

When I began to work with the conference committee, I told committee members "about my research interests, and asked if it was OK to include them in my notes" (FN, 02/26). They agreed to this, and later agreed to my tape recording the committee meetings. I had hoped that some committee members would form a research group with me, but no one responded when I suggested this. The committee wanted to organize a conference; the research was my interest.

As I started the research, I knew that I wanted to learn about sharing power. Rather than pose a specific question, I collected information with this general focus in mind. By the end of the conference project, I had a number of sources to work with.

How I Collected Information

Field notes. As soon as possible after each meeting, I wrote up my recollections, observations and reflections about what happened. When I was able to take notes during the meetings, I incorporated these into my write-up. Sometimes I added questions and reminders about points to take up in the next meeting.

Tape recordings. About a month into the project, I asked if I could tape record committee meetings. I felt that the tape recordings would be a more accurate record of the proceedings than my field notes might be. I hadn't asked to tape at the start, as I felt that the tape recorder would be too intrusive. For the same reason, I did not tape a particular meeting that revolved around a conflict. As I started to tape, I kept notes less frequently and my notes focused more on my thoughts and questions. I transcribed most of the tapes myself, and hired someone to transcribe others because of time constraints.

Presentations about the conference project. The committee made three public presentations about the conference project: to a university class, at the conference itself, and at a provincial literacy conference. The scripts for these presentations provided another source of information.

To help the committee prepare for the first presentation, I used a process similar to a language experience activity to help us recall and describe what we had done (Campbell, 1994). The process was also similar to a semi-structured interview, as I posed questions to prompt recall or elicit points of view.

As we recalled activities, I acted as scribe, recording on a flip chart what committee members said. After we reviewed and revised the text, I typed it up for further review and revision. I suggested formatting the presentation as a script, and people chose parts to read. The script was revised and updated for subsequent presentations, and eventually included in the conference publication, *Students Meeting Students* (2000).

Interviews. At my request, Grace Malicky interviewed four of the committee members at the end of the conference project, in order to provide another perspective on my work with the committee. I prepared the interview questions and suggested four people to interview, based on who was available and who seemed at ease talking with a relative outsider. I hoped that people would feel that they could criticize my actions, although Grace suggested that no matter how friendly my relationship with them, people would still feel constrained because of my position as coordinator. To try to address this, Grace had the interview tapes transcribed, collated the transcripts, and did not name people in the collation. However, because I am familiar with participants' speech patterns and experiences, it is hard for me not to identify the speakers. In some cases, comments were critical, and I recognize and appreciate that people may have been uncomfortable, even somewhat fearful about making them. I have no way of knowing if some people avoided critical comments because of discomfort or fear, or because they really did not have any criticisms to offer. (Interview questions are included in Appendix B.)

Consent and Confidentiality

At the end of our work on the conference, I asked people to sign consent forms, indicating whether I could include their words and ideas in my analysis and write-up. I waited until the end of the project to request this consent, so that people would have a better idea of what they were agreeing to. By this time, one person was no longer attending The Learning Centre, so I omitted reference to this individual from my analysis.

Everyone who signed consent forms said they wanted me to use their first names in my writing. I feel that this is a way to acknowledge and celebrate people's contributions to the conference. However, names are not used with quotes from Grace's interviews and I also decided not to use names when describing situations that potentially cast people in a negative light. The purpose of describing the situations is to gain insights about sharing power, not to spotlight individuals.

When I reviewed my writing with committee members, I asked if they wanted any descriptions or quotes omitted, and whether and when to use their names. I also relied on Grace, as research mentor, to advise me about whether and when I was crossing ethical boundaries.

How I Made Sense of the Information

> There is no clear and accepted set of conventions for [qualitative] analysis corresponding to those observed with quantitative data. (Robson, 1993, p. 370)

Analysis of information began almost as soon as I started to collect it. As I wrote field notes, I included questions and ideas about what I was documenting. Through ongoing reading, I found a framework for understanding power. When I made time to work more intensely and intentionally on the analysis, I used this framework as a starting point.

I went through all of my field notes and Grace's summary of interviews, highlighting parts that seemed to relate to the framework and my research focus. I began to think about how bits of highlighted information related to each other, and started to add headings to categorize the information.

I sorted the highlighted bits according to the headings I'd made, then resorted and adjusted headings. Meanwhile, I re-read materials that had helped me identify a framework for understanding power. I revised my understanding of the readings based on the information I'd analysed. I re-sorted information and reviewed the transcripts of taped meetings, as a check against my field notes. As I wrote about my learnings, I continued to go back and forth between my information, the readings, and my writing. Gradually I built an understanding about my attempts to share power with the conference committee. I reviewed my research report with committee members and incorporated their elaborations into a revision.

A Framework for Understanding Power

Publications by Starhawk (1987) and Cranton (1994) provided an initial framework for me to examine and learn from my efforts to share power. Starhawk writes about three kinds of power: power-over, power-with and power-from-within.

Power-over is often thought of in terms of persons, groups or institutions having power over others. Such power is sustained by social, political and economic systems and by policies and assumptions about which groups have a right to power. These assumptions are often reflected in prevailing discourses, which help sustain existing power relations.

Horsman (1990) explains discourse as the complex set of language, meanings and assumptions that shape our understanding and influence our actions. As an example, I use the term student in this paper, because that is the term people use at The Learning Centre. Use of the term student reflects dominant understandings that align literacy programs with schools—in fact many people who come to the Centre refer to it as "the school." In alternate discourses, programs might be writing groups or reading clubs, and those who attend might be named participants or members.

Cranton writes about a particular form of power-over, namely the position power of an educator. In my position as paid coordinator and facilitator at The Learning Centre I have certain formal authority and control. As well, because of common discourses about school, teachers and students, I am accorded "teacher" power. Such factors as my Anglo-Norman heritage and my middle class language, education and income provide access to power in many contexts outside of the

Centre. These factors intersect with the position power I have at the Centre.

Cranton distinguishes between position power and the personal power that educators—and students—have in the form of skills, knowledge, personal attributes and attitudes. Personal power shifts into power-with, or sharing power, when others both value and are open to receiving what is being offered. According to Starhawk, power-with is one's influence in a group. It is "the power of a strong individual in a group of equals, the power not to command, but to suggest and be listened to . . . " (p. 10). Power-with is based in respect, not for the role or position, but for the person.

As I interpret them, personal power is a related but different concept from power-from-within. Power-from-within has to do with being able to say, "I can"; it a belief in ourselves and our capacities that enables us to use and further develop our skills, knowledge and attributes, and to offer them to others.

Learnings

Sharing power with the conference committee required the students and me to share and develop our personal power—to draw on the skills and attributes we had and learn new ones. As personal power was offered and accepted, power-from-within also grew, in turn making it easier for the students and me to share personal power and influence. In order for us to share power, however, we needed to learn alternatives to power-over.

In the following sections, I describe my learnings about power-over, about shifting to power-with and about students reclaiming power-from-within.

Learning about Power-over

Early in the project I tried to devolve power to the committee. As I met with resistance, I realized that in trying to transfer power, I was still exercising power-over. Later in the project, a particular incident revealed how I used position power to manipulate decision making. Another incident reminded me that at times I do have to exercise the authority and responsibility of my position as a program coordinator. In this section, I talk about devolution. I return to other learnings about power-over later in the paper.

Devolution

Near the start of the student conference project, I was invited to help facilitate a literacy conference in eastern Canada. I arranged funding for two students to attend with me. I thought that attending the conference would be an opportunity for students to travel, meet other people and learn about a different kind of conference. (Rather than offering speaker presentations and workshops, the proposed conference would engage participants in workshops and discussions about literacy practices.)

In a morning meeting, I told the committee about the eastern conference and suggested that a selection committee be formed to choose two people to attend. Over the lunch hour, I was told that students were talking about the eastern conference and feeling that I should choose who should go. When the committee revisited the matter in the afternoon

> The notion came out that students felt there would be hard feelings if students made the selection. I asked why it would be different if I did—the reply was that it would be accepted more, I was the boss [implied, not said]. (FN, 02/23)

Students who were interviewed had similar recall of the developments. As one commented,

> *I said, it's not going to be fair to anybody else because there's going to be a lot of people who really want to go, right, and there's going to be hard feelings. Say Mary took [another student] and I. . . . Then the rest of the students would be kind of like, well, why do they get to go and we don't? So that was, like no, forget it Mary, we're not going to . . . help anybody choose.* (Interview)

Despite feedback, I persisted with the idea of having a group select people to go to the eastern conference. Then, in the afternoon meeting,

> I suddenly realized what a request I was making of the students who might serve on a selection committee. I pulled back and noted that we were talking about power here, I realized that I had the power to choose (although I hadn't thought of it that way). . . . At the same time I indicated that I wasn't prepared to chose, that this was an opportunity for people to learn. (FN, 02/23)

I chose the term devolution to capture the meaning of these proceedings. Like governments that pass on power and responsibilities to community agencies, I was trying to pass on power to the conference committee. I had not consulted with them about whether they wanted this power, nor whether they were prepared to accept and exercise it. Starhawk notes that

> an empowering group does not thrust responsibilities on people without preparation, but creates situations in which information, skills, and the knowledge gained by experience can be passed on. (p. 272)

At this stage in working with the committee, I was standing back. Lil noted, in a meeting with a visitor, "I think Mary wants us to do it ourselves" (FN, 02/02). I still had to learn that I could share my knowledge and skills, as well as how to share them. At the same time, I had to learn how to invite others to identify, develop and share theirs.

I see now, that in asking students to choose delegates, I was merely trying to make a shift in who had power-over, rather than initiate a shift to power-with. Work by Wheeler and Chinn (1991) reminded me that I had been raised, educated and employed in patriarchal contexts where power and authority is distributed hierarchically and power-over is the norm. So, in retrospect, it is not surprising that I was influenced by patriarchal/hierarchical discourses of power.

At the same time, if students on the conference committee had mainly experienced power-over in educational and other settings, it may have been hard for them to conceive of other forms of power. Students on the committee also identified strongly with each other. In the follow-up interviews, one student responded:

> I figured Mary should have made [the decision] herself. Because if us students were in it, there would have been a lot of difficulties. . . . Because there would have been hard feelings and nobody would have been talking to nobody. . . . I think anything like that where Mary wants to take students she should pick . . . because we're too close. It's like living in a family.

If some students accepted the role of choosing conference delegates, they would be seen as having power over—of being one of "them" rather than one of "us."

Shifting to Power-with

Arnold et al. (1991) note that while educators need to acknowledge differences between them and students, these differences don't necessarily have to get in the way. In order for students and me to share power, we needed opportunities to get to know each other and develop personal relationships. When this happened, bridges across power differences started to form, we began to share influence, and I learned about providing responsive leadership. In the process, I learned the importance of listening and about understanding silences.

Developing relationships/Taking time to be

Other committee members had developed friendly relationships with each other. Some were in the women's group together, some had attended the same conferences, most took their breaks together, and some saw each other socially outside of the program. I had tended to be friendly enough with students, but to keep a professional distance. In retrospect, this distance may have made it difficult for people to see me other than as the teacher. My relationship with other committee members began to change through events I call "road trips."

Following the eastern conference discussion, described earlier, I suggested that the committee could use the expense funds for another purpose. We decided to hold a residential conference so a number of people could get away, rather than just two. Helen contacted some potential conference sites and I assumed that three or four people, including me as driver, would visit these sites on behalf of the committee. However, more than three or four wanted to go. Based on my earlier experience, I wasn't prepared to choose people or initiate a selection process. I suggested that we ask another Learning Centre staff person to drive as well.

On the drive to and from the sites, as well as during the tours, there was plenty of time to chat and listen in groups and one-to-one. Later, in preparing for a presentation about the conference project,

> I asked about whether things had changed, or about my role. . . . Somewhere I also commented that people seemed more comfortable about saying what they really thought. . . . Lil said "We feel more comfortable now. You're one of the group. We can joke around." I asked her why she hadn't felt this way before, she hesitated, then said it was just a gut feeling. (FN, 03/26)

I noted

> Lil's comments were interesting in light of my own inner debates about boundaries and my relationship with people. Maybe as long as I stay aloof I will be the "teacher." Maybe there needs to be a certain degree of familiarity before we can interact easily. (FN, 03/26)

Cranton suggests that personal power is increased when educators become real persons to learners and feelings of friendship and loyalty develop. Taking time to "be," through the road trip, was a step in this process.

Campbell (1994) introduces the difference between "being" and "doing," based on research about participatory practices in student groups. She found that while students saw groups as a time to be with other students, practitioners were concerned about what student groups would do. Campbell notes that opportunities to relax and discuss may be limited for people who work in labouring jobs, compared to those in professions. People who are not working may also be isolated from others and educational programs provide one venue where people can meet and talk. My own focus on doing reflects my alliance with a society that is concerned with doing; it also reflected the fact that I have other occasions to be and don't need to do that in my work context. The site visit offered opportunities for both students and me to be and enabled all of us to become real persons to each other.

Towards sharing influence

Starhawk notes that influence may never be entirely equalized, because "some people do have experience or skills or imagination that a group finds consistently of value, and their opinions do carry weight" (p. 268). I came to understand that we committee members had different capacities to influence, depending on the context. The first road trip was an authentic opportunity for committee members to share skills and influence. Helen contacted conference sites and made appointments. Tammy asked another staff person to drive. We all joined in touring the centres and committee members took the lead in asking questions about the facilities, referring to the list of questions we'd made beforehand. Afterwards, Helen wrote thank-you notes to staff at the conference sites. In many ways, my main role during the site visits was as a chauffeur.

Selecting a site was not unlike finding an apartment or house to rent (Mary, presentation). Thus, the task was familiar enough that committee members were able to exercise influence by drawing on their experiences—their personal power. In retrospect, I had been intuitively inviting students to share their "outside of school" skills since I started working at The Learning Centre. For example, students had planned socials, cooked, greeted people, painted and done repairs. Yet, somehow I overlooked the value of drawing on such skills as we started to plan the conference.

Committee members had many experiences and skills to contribute to the conference project. They also learned new skills. Gradually, I recognized that one of my roles was to invite and support committee members to develop and use their skills, through responsive leadership.

Responsive leadership

A shift to power-with had started to occur when Helen, one of the committee members, began to chair the committee meetings. When the conference project started, I asked if anyone wanted to chair the next meeting. Helen had volunteered, noting that she had some experience chairing meetings in another group. However, at the next meeting Helen was feeling low due to a family member's death, so I chaired. I continued to chair meetings until three weeks later, when "somehow or other I remembered that Helen said she was interested in chairing meetings. . . . I asked Helen if she still wanted to chair and she said yes" (FN, 03/02). With Helen in the chair, I started to feel ". . . like a member of the group." I also noticed that there was "more interaction among people when Helen is chairing . . . "(FN, 03/09).

In retrospect, transferring the chair's position to a student was another form of devolution. The concept of chairperson relates to hierarchical models of meetings and decision making, and my actions were still influenced by these models. However, Helen was keen to accept the role of chair and to learn skills to carry it out. As well, Helen's chairing was a visible example that a student could have influence:

> *Helen is chairing, she has more experience than most of us. It makes us feel good that a student could do that. We supported her, we could understand and help out.* (Lil, presentation)

Helen and I generally prepared meeting agendas together. Helen opened meetings and guided the committee through the agenda. During meetings I coached Helen about meeting process. In the first meeting

> I reminded her to review the agenda and to tell the newcomers what we had planned so far. . . . [When a question came up] I suggested she ask people to give reasons for their answers—I could see Helen becoming more adept at asking people this as she went around the circle. (FN, 03/05)

Field notes and meeting transcripts show that I continued to coach Helen throughout the conference project. Sometimes I facilitated when a topic being discussed was complex or emotionally charged.

> Sometimes Helen is more of a scribe as I take on the facilitating. . . . This has happened a couple of times now . . . particularly when there is work to be done. (FN, 04/09)

> Some people started to talk about whether we could bring friends, where we would have tickets made, etc. I find that when this happens I tend to jump in. I suggested that we needed to decide first of all if we wanted to have an open event or if we wanted it just for students at the conference. I suggested to Helen that she ask people to suggest reasons for either kind of event and to list them on the board. (FN, 04/09)

I debated with and sometimes berated myself for jumping in or taking over. However, Starhawk's writing suggests that in coaching and facilitating I was exercising "responsive leadership." She uses this term to identify "power-with or influence used to empower the group and individuals in it" (p. 270). According to Starhawk, responsive leaders train others by providing models or challenging them to stretch their skills.

During the conference project, other committee members carried out various roles and in doing so, contributed their personal power to the group. In some cases, people responded to opportunities to take on a task and drew on previous experiences to complete it. In other instances, people needed invitations and various kinds of support. This seems obvious, but it was a while before I realized that I needed to help some people find ways to be involved.

> I really haven't figured out what to do regarding Tammy's involvement. . . . I need to think about some concrete things she could be doing (FN).

> I had copied the agenda on the board so Helen could have a break. In future I might suggest that Tammy do this—copy it after Helen/I have drafted it. (FN)

While attempting to encourage students to take on tasks, I also struggled with balancing my interest in having conference materials meet my standards and not taking over a role or task from the person doing it. The following describes my work with Kathy as she prepared to call coordinators of other literacy programs about the conference.

> I sat with her and helped her rehearse. Although I was giving a lot of input in the form of questions, etc., Kathy composed

sentences and scribed them . . . then she called. Kathy got more confident as she went along and was quite excited about the responses. I'm not sure that she would have been able to do it entirely on her own. I know though that I was there to support Kathy, rather than out of concern about how we come across to the other coordinators. I think that may have been on my mind at one time. (FN, 02/23)

Other committee members also provided support and challenge so that everyone experienced having influence and being listened to at some times. I observed Lil inviting other committee members to take on tasks and noticed how some committee members who had greater capacity to influence would step back so others had a chance to experience and learn.

While I and others tried to challenge and support committee members in their chosen roles, one member who was interviewed felt that she hadn't received enough encouragement or support.

> *So Mary said, well I was supposed to be on the registration but then [name] she took over . . . so I said, "Well, where's my part to fit in there?" So I didn't bother . . . cause I knew I could do the registration. And at the end of it, I started working on it again . . . but I sort of had problems. So I had to learn on my own and I kept [staff person] there with me to make sure I was doing everything right. . . . I had to learn everything on my own and that's one thing I think really upset me.* (Interview)

I had assumed that this committee member had experience and skills both to stretch into a role and to speak up about taking it on. As other committee members were encouraged and supported to develop and exercise personal power, this committee member may have felt a loss of influence.

> *I know I'm supposed to do something, I'm always there to do it and then when somebody else took over, that's where I felt left out.* (Interview)

Understanding silence/Learning to listen

Sharing power in the conference project meant that students had to speak and be heard. However, there were times during the project when students did not speak or I did not hear them when they did.

When I first attempted to devolve power to the committee, students voiced their responses among themselves rather than raising them in a meeting with me. In retrospect, given the familiar discourse of school and my position power in relation to the committee, this silence is not surprising. Ellsworth (1989) suggests that differences in people's power will consciously or unconsciously influence their decisions to speak. To speak up at the meeting would have meant publicly disagreeing with me.

Creating safe environments where people can risk speaking in spite of power differences is essential if power is to be shared (Arnold et al., 1991; Campbell, 1994). In the devolution incident, I did nothing to invite dialogue or to make it safe and comfortable for people to express their views. Later, I successfully invited response to the idea of choosing delegates to the eastern conference, but I did not listen to people's concerns. Instead I persisted with my agenda. Yet, listening is also fundamental to participatory education:

> To listen is to be on an equal footing: listening means putting yourself into the place of the other. How can educators construct a setting in which there isn't a growing "we versus them," no matter how genuine our intent to do otherwise? . . . the art of listening is an important pillar in building structures that counteract some deeply ingrained, top-down teaching habits. (Arnold et al., 1991, p. 162)

As well as listening to what people did say, I had to learn to listen to other silences in order to understand and address what they meant. Events during the conference project helped me understand that people may be silent because they don't know what to say, that they don't understand me, or that they are nervous or afraid.

We don't know what to say. While planning the conference agenda, the committee decided to have table groups as a way for students to meet students. Groups would meet for 15 minutes and talk about a topic related to their programs and learning. Some of the committee members expressed interest in facilitating these groups. To help people prepare, I planned some sessions on facilitation.

At one of these sessions, it seemed to me that people were not interested. When I raised this after the break ". . . Mary said that sometimes they just don't know what to say" (FN, n.d.). I realized that in the discussion,

> people haven't had enough experience yet to have more ideas about what to do in certain situations. Maybe there is a need for more direct instruction, bringing in information, presenting ideas, etc. rather than always asking, "What do you do [when] . . . ?" (FN, 05/18)

To address lack of experience, I suggested that interested committee members interview some staff and volunteers about their experiences as facilitators. A group of three developed a questionnaire and each interviewed someone (see Appendix C). The collected responses provided guidelines for the new facilitators. Perhaps as important, the interview process placed students in positions of influence, as they were the ones posing the questions.

Not understanding. In the interviews, one of the students commented that *I had a lot of education* but that I was able to *come down to [the students'] level.* (Being familiar with students' talk, I'm fairly sure she meant I communicated clearly, not that I was condescending.) However, there were times, such as during the session on facilitation, when I was not clear. At first, I confused students' not understanding with disinterest.

> During the first half of the meeting, I was starting to ask myself "Why am I doing this?" I was aware of those feelings, and I think in part they were a response to my feeling of ineptitude—not knowing what to do. I had not considered that the content/process was "above people's heads"—I was thinking they were not interested—but how can you be interested when you really don't know what is going on? I wonder how many times some of the group have checked out because they didn't know what was going on. (FN, 05/08)

Being nervous. In the session about facilitation, "Mary or Lil said something about how everyone was starting to feel a little afraid of what was going to happen—what if they said something wrong, etc." (FN, 05/18). Following their lead, I introduced a concrete, engaging activity to help us imagine a successful conference. We brainstormed what we hoped people would learn, how they would feel and what they might do after attending the conference. Confidence and energy was boosted, but I still had some learning to do about recognizing silence as a sign of nervousness.

After completing their interviews about facilitation, Linda and Holly had agreed that they would practise facilitating a small group. As we reviewed the questions they were going to ask

> Holly gave a big sigh and threw her hands in her lap. My first response was, "She's not interested, she doesn't want to do this —How's she going to do it if she doesn't practise . . . ?" Around this time, Linda said, "I don't think I want to do this," or "I don't want to go through with this." Again I realized that they were both getting "scared." (FN, 05/21)

After we talked about the fears, Linda and Holly decided to go ahead with the practice. The practice sessions went smoothly and their facilitation at the conference was a smashing success.

Reclaiming Power-from-within

All of these forms of silence had to do with power relations, whether between me and the committee or between committee members and others (Campbell, 1994, 1996). In responding to my research report, Holly commented that she had been nervous about facilitating because she hadn't realized that the people coming to the conference "were like us, having trouble learning." She was silenced by assumptions that conference delegates would have more education and use their position to judge her. To break silences required Holly and the others to draw on power-from-within.

As the committee continued to work together, some students started to feel more able to speak up.

> *If I didn't know something, or the other students didn't know something, I asked her to explain it to us, and she wouldn't disappoint us.* (Interview)

This student went on to explain that if she wasn't understanding something, she knew that other students weren't. She broke the silence by asking what I was talking about and paved the way for others. Eventually, all the committee members had public opportunities to speak and be heard, especially at the conference. As they were listened to and heard, they experienced sharing power.

In responding to my research report, Holly and Mary talked about speaking up in situations where they used to be silent:

> *I used to be like that. If you don't speak up, people will walk all over you.* (Holly)

Learning More About Power-over

As I began to experience sharing power-with, I also began to recognize instances when my efforts to share power were actually subtle forms of using power-over. I became aware of hidden leadership and manipulation as forms of exercising power-over.

Hidden leadership

I can identify many instances in which I coached or facilitated, and in interviews students commented that I helped them learn skills. However, in relation to Helen's role as chair, students summed my role up in terms of being there if they needed me. They also hinted that Helen, as chair, could have done the job on her own.

> *Well, the difference between Helen and Mary was, Mary was there when we needed her. Helen was there all the time. She actually chaired this conference committee and chaired the conference . . . and she did a really good job. She probably could have done it herself but it was actually a little bit better that Mary was there just in case we needed some, really needed help from her.* (Interview)

While students acknowledged my "being there", they seemed to value my scribing role as much, if not more:

> *She was the one that did all the writing for us, anything we said she wrote down, then she kept all the notes. . . . Because then it would really be done properly. . . . I think a lot of us students were scared we'd miss a lot of what the students, other students were saying. . . . I would've just taken down what I thought was important for myself.* (Interview)

> *She kept the notes for us and then when we'd get stuck, she'd provide it through the notes for us and say, "Oh, you said this or you said that." . . . If we didn't have those notes, I don't know what we would have done.* (Interview)

Perhaps my scribing role was more visible than my coaching and facilitating roles. Sometimes I commented that I felt I was taking over and asked people to let me know if I was being too pushy (FN, 02/23). However, on the whole, my facilitating may have been invisible. Starhawk suggests that hidden leadership is the worst kind of leadership because leaders who are not acknowledged cannot be held accountable for their actions.

In most cases, I believe, my hidden leadership was benevolent. I purposely stayed behind the scenes so others could experience being on the stage. However, sometimes my hidden leadership, while well intended, was actually forms of manipulation.

Manipulation

Arnstein (1969) suggests that manipulation is a form of non-participation that substitutes for genuine participation and enables "power holders to 'educate' participants or engineer their support" (p. 217). I use the term manipulation to describe situations where I had an agenda or idea but did not state it. Rather, I used questions and discussion until people came around to my way of thinking.

In some cases, I asked questions, hoping that participants would give the "right" answers. For example, after the discussion about the eastern conference, I suggested to the group that we could continue with that plan, or use the expense money for something else. I had in mind that the funds could be used for the student conference.

After one of the committee members suggested that the money came to the Centre for field trips or similar activities, I introduced the idea of using it to have the conference at another site. People began to talk about a trip—going camping, getting away, no stress, etc. This was before I realized the importance of taking time to be, so

> I was doing some mental gymnastics—should I let it go this way, or would I bring it back to "my agenda." I realized that I felt really uncomfortable with the idea of "just a trip." So, I told people this—explained that I was in that position again, how I had some questions about "just a trip," but wasn't sure if I should go along with the idea or say that we had to do a conference. Was it the LC's business to be providing "trips" for people? OR should it include some times for people to read, write, communicate, learn, etc. (FN, 02/26)

Despite the process, there did seem to be consensus about the outcome. Interview transcripts support my interpretation:

> *So we told Mary . . . put that money in our student conference and that's what she did.*

As I recognized this habit of asking leading questions, I began to state my views directly. Usually, my ideas were taken up or not, depending on whether people valued them. However, there was at least one incident where people agreed to my view, not because they valued it, but because of my position.

The incident occurred about three months into the conference project. A student who had not been on the committee decided to come to a meeting. Up to this point, the committee had not talked about whether or when people might join the committee, although others had been welcomed to meetings. After the newcomer left the meeting, committee members were clear and strong in stating their views that she not join the committee. While some suggested it would be hard for her to catch up, others focused on interactions they had observed or experienced with her. I summarized discussion and then introduced my view:

> I talked about my own belief that if we expect people to behave well or in good ways, and support them, they will. So we could just say no, or we could see if she responded to being welcomed. (FN, 05/20)

After more discussion, some committee members began to soften, noting, *It's so hard to say no* and *I'll help her catch up*. However, one member was clearly opposed: *My answer is still no....* I then talked about options, "We could say no, we could say yes, or we could give it a try and have some expectations." At this point, the person who had expressed strong opposition said, *I think I could go along with this* (FN, 05/20).

At one point in the meeting, I had actually said that I was hesitant to express my views because I didn't want to influence people. Yet it is quite evident from my notes that I persisted until everyone agreed that the newcomer could join the committee. Committee members who were interviewed were asked to comment on my role in the decision.

> *It was actually the rest of the conference committee's decision because . . . Mary couldn't, I mean Mary could say, "Yeah, sure [name] you could join" and then the rest of us conference committee people . . . didn't really want her in there. . . . So she left it up to us if we wanted her or not. So we chose, we said, "Okay."* (Interview)

> *That was a tough one . . . it was a hard decision to make. . . . It was really tough for Mary so she brought it to us. . . . I think some of them didn't want her to come in but we figured, well, she's a student here so may as well give her a chance.* (Interview)

While the outcome of this meeting reflected my wishes, the meeting differed from the earlier one in terms of how people participated in discussion. Most committee members seemed able to voice their views, once the newcomer had left. By this time, my relationship with the group had developed and people may have felt safer about speaking out. However, my position power may have silenced some:

> *When everybody said no, it should have been left there. . . . But the students, a lot of them wasn't happy. They meant no, but they said yes because they didn't want to say no to Mary. . . . I think*

*Mary should have discussed it with the students and she should
have let the students make up their own decision.* (Interview)

In reviewing this incident, I am aware that the committee and I were
still operating from a power-over perspective. Whether it was the
committee as a whole or I who influenced the decision, we were still at
some level exercising power-over the newcomer.

Exercising power openly

During the conference a situation arose which prompted me to ask a
person attending the conference to leave. Under other circumstances I
might have involved committee members in deciding action. I felt there
wasn't time for such discussion during the conference and further, that
such discussion would upset and distract people from carrying out
their conference roles.

When interviewed about this incident, most committee members
concurred with the decision and how it was made.

> *I think that was good what she did because I think it would have
> upset us at the Bennett Centre. If she would have said, "Well, we're
> going to have a little meeting before we start the workshops," I
> don't think we would have concentrated so well on our work at the
> conference.* (Interview)

Clearly, however, I acted hierarchically. Reflecting on this event helped
to clarify that I have position power within a hierarchical structure.
Looking back, I also became conscious of the contrast between this
situation and the event described just before. In one situation I used
my position power to include, in the other it was to exclude.

Applying Learnings to Practice

> Critical research attempts to uncover the systems that underlie
> social relationships and to understand the causes of social
> tensions and conflicts. Through critical research people can
> come to understand and try to change "supposed" natural
> constraints. Critical research can also be used to help people
> see themselves and their situations in new ways. This
> understanding can help inform further action for self-directed
> emancipation from oppressive social systems and relationships.
> The dialectical relationship between research and action is an
> important aspect of critical research. (Winberg, 1997, p. 21)

It is hard to believe that almost two years have passed since the conference committee hosted the Students Meeting Students event. Six of the committee members and I continue to learn, teach and be with others at The Learning Centre. Mary and Lil are now employed at the Centre part-time, Mary as a teaching assistant and Lil as a co-facilitator of the women's group.

Learnings from my research have affected how I see myself and my situation. They continue to frame how I approach my practice, reflection, and related writing, and may offer suggestions for others who aim to teach and learn in participatory ways.

Accepting and Devolving Position Power

In all my work now, I am more conscious and accepting that as a full-time paid coordinator, I have different authority, responsibilities and power than the part-time staff, volunteers and learners. As much as I and others at the Centre try to share power within the program, the Centre operates within a hierarchical system. I am also more aware and accepting of my personal power and capacity to influence. Given this awareness, I now try to ask myself, "How can I use my power responsibly and responsively—while also sharing power when possible and appropriate?"

Distinguishing between devolving and sharing power was a key learning for me, as was recognizing the influence of the discourse of patriarchal power. I have continued to devolve position power to Centre participants, but have first asked if they wanted this power and the accompanying responsibilities. I have also tried to provide support as needed and hope that I have encouraged people to use power-with approaches.

For example, the provincial literacy association has granted bursaries for students to attend its annual conference. For a number of years, all applicants from The Learning Centre—as many as ten or more per year—had been approved. In 1999, the bursary program was changed and programs were asked to select and submit no more than four applications. I asked some participants from the conference committee to review applications and select delegates. Using their knowledge of conferences, they developed selection criteria and used them to make their choices. Although somewhat "sad" about having to turn down some applicants, they seemed confident about making the choices and about accepting responsibility for them.

Talking about Power

When the conference committee started, students wanted to *do something themselves* (Holly) and I wanted to learn about sharing power. While we expressed these goals, we didn't talk about what either of them meant for us. I'm not sure we really knew. Based on what I learned, I am more intentional about naming and working with power related concepts.

I have used Starhawk's (1989) framework to encourage analysis of power relations in my work with participants at the Centre, as well as in workshops with other practitioners. For example, when some participants at the Centre identified "speaking up" as a learning goal, I used Starhawk's framework to plan some workshops. We read and shared stories about not speaking up because of fearing what a boss, spouse or bully—people with power–over—might do. We then discussed ways to reclaim power-from-within, with the support of others (power-with).

I have also started to use the framework to invite discussion about power relations and influence among participants at the Centre. I am sure that people are aware of differences in their personal power and influence, yet the differences are rarely named. Rather, they are hidden behind notions of being "too close . . . like a family."

Preparing to Share Power

Sharing power requires group members to share personal power— abilities, interests, talents and knowledge. I have observed how groups in other settings identify and list what each person can contribute. A process like this would have been helpful at the start of the conference project. As well, I could have encouraged people to list what they wanted to learn. We could have returned to the lists periodically to add newly identified or learned abilities. I plan to introduce such a process in future projects. Processes for sharing power in meetings, such as taking turns as chairperson, could also be introduced (Wheeler and Chinn, 1991).

Taking Time to Be

The road trips were instrumental in inviting power-with by providing time to develop personal relationships. Since the conference project,

The Learning Centre has had annual getaways for students, community volunteers and staff. The first year after the conference, 30 Centre members spent two days at a comfortable camp outside the city. A talented facilitator provided an engaging structure to help us get to know each other as we sang, created a mural, ate, and "recreated."

Resisting Power-over

Rodriguez (1993) suggests that power-over can be exercised effectively only if individuals or groups submit to this power. In theory, when people resist submission, power-over loses its effectiveness. Starhawk (1987) explains resistance by contrasting it with rebellion. Rebellion involves defying a reality, but resistance includes the presentation of alternatives to that reality.

My learnings with the student conference committee strengthened my beliefs that literacy programs can offer alternatives to common experiences of power-over and the discourses that explain and support it. Programs can be places where learners, volunteers and staff experience more equitable power relations. With these experiences, we may see new possibilities for resisting power-over and creating more equitable relations outside programs.

My research would not have happened without the other committee members' tenacity, courage and desire to see the conference project through, and I thank them.

References

Arnold, R., Barndt, D., & Burke, B. (1985). *A new weave: Popular education in Canada and Central America.* Toronto, ON: Canadian University Services Overseas Development Education and Ontario Institute for Studies in Education.

Arnold, R., Burke, B., James, C., Martin, D. & Thomas, B. (1991). *Educating for a change.* Toronto, ON: Between the Lines and the Doris Marshall Institute for Education and Action.

Arnstein, S. (1969, July). A ladder of citizenship participation. *AIP Journal,* 216–224.

Auerbach, E. (1993). Putting the P back in participatory. *TESOL Quarterly, 27,* 543-45.

Campbell, P. (1994). *Participatory literacy practices. Having a voice, having a vote.* Unpublished doctoral dissertation, University of Toronto, Toronto.

Campbell, P. (1994). Participatory literacy practices: Exploring social identity and relations. *Adult Basic Education, 6,* 127–142.

Cranton, P. A. (1996). *Understanding and promoting transformative learning.* San Francisco: Jossey Bass.

Ellsworth, E. (1989). Why doesn't this feel empowering? Working through the repressive myths of critical pedagogy. *Harvard Educational Review, 59*(3), 297-324.

Gaber-Katz, E., & Watson, G. M. (1991). *The land that we dream of: A participatory study of community-based literacy.* Toronto, ON: OISE.

Hamilton, M. (1989, Summer). What is research? *RaPAL Bulletin, 9,* 5–6.

Horsman, J. (1990). *Something on my mind besides the everyday.* Toronto, ON: Women's Press, 1990.

Hull, G. (1993). Hearing other voices: A critical assessment of popular views on literacy and work. *Harvard Educational Review,* 63(1), 20–50.

Jurmo, P. (1989). The case for participatory literacy education. *New Directions for Continuing Education, 42,*17–34.

Merrifield, J. (1999). Literacy, community and citizenship: What do we teach, how do we teach it? Reflections from US experiences. *RaPAL Bulletin, 38,* 3–6.

Norton, M. (1996). *Getting our own education: Learning about participatory education in an adult learning centre.* Edmonton, AB: The Learning Centre Literacy Association.

Robson, C. (1993). *Real world research: A resource for social scientists and practitioner researchers.* Oxford, UK: Blackwell.

Rodriguez, C. (1993). *Educating for change: Community-based student centred literacy programming with First Nations adults.* Salmon Arm, BC: K'noowenchoot Aboriginal Adult Education Resources, Okanagan College.

Ross, J. A. (1997). Popular education: An alternative strategy for health promotion with women. FES *Occasional Paper Series, 3*(5). Toronto, ON: York University.

Starhawk. (1987). *Truth or dare: Encounters with power, authority and mystery.* San Francisco: Harper.

Students meeting students. Putting a student conference together. (2000). Edmonton, AB: Voices Rising/Learning at the Centre Press.

Wheeler, C. E., & Chinn, P. L. (1991). *Peace and power: A handbook of feminist process.* New York: National League for Nursing.

Winberg, C. (1997). *Learning how to research and evaluate.* Cape Town: Juta.

Appendix A

Ways that students said they participate at The Learning Centre

When asked about participation in The Learning Centre, a group of students identified a range of ways. These included:

- choosing our own books
- helping each other, showing each other what we do, tutoring
- help mail English Express
- active in AAAL conference
- we decide what we want to do
- giving feedback
- socializing
- students volunteering
- attending
- asking for help when we need it
- decide what groups we need
- people on the board, we have students who talk for us
- staff listens to suggestions
- sharing, encouraging victories
- trying out computers, try new things
- communicating with each other
- contribute to the newsletter, Writer
- reception
- respect each other
- we share our writing and we ask for feedback
- listen, laugh, get along with each other
- practise on your own
- to get to be equal, teacher can learn from the student
- it goes both ways, students have to give input, coordinators go on that

Appendix B

Interview conducted at the end of the conference project

Questions/Topics

- What was Mary's role with the conference committee? Did the committee need her to work with you? If so, what did you need her for?

- What was the same or different between Helen's and Mary's jobs?

- What were some things Mary did that helped the committee in the meetings?

- What were some things Mary did that did not help the committee?

- What did Mary do to help you with your tasks on the committee?

- What could Mary do in the future to help more?

- Decision making—the choice of students to go to the eastern conference

- The decision to let new people join the committee

- The decision to ask someone leave the conference

Appendix C

Being a facilitator
Interview Introduction and Questions

We are having a conference for students to meet other students. Some students from The Learning Centre will be facilitators. We are talking to people about how they do their job as a facilitator.

1. How long have you been a facilitator?

2. How did you become a facilitator?

3. What is a facilitator's responsibilities?

4. What are some of the challenges?

5. How do you deal with them [the challenges]?

6. What do you do when people don't listen?

7. Some of us are worried about saying the right thing. How do you deal with this?

8. Is there anything you would like to tell us about being a facilitator?

Chapter 9

Why Don't People Come? Some Reasons for Non-participation in Literacy Programs

Veronica Park

Veronica Park

Why Don't People Come? Some Reasons for Non-participation in Literacy Programs

I work in a community literacy program in a small city that is the urban centre for an agricultural area. We offer several streams of service, including one-to-one volunteer tutoring for adult literacy and English as a Second Language learners, Reading Pals for elementary school students, and family literacy programs. We also offer a small group class in English as a Second Language.

In 1998, a review of the demographics of the community indicated that, when benchmarked against provincial statistical data, the population tended to fall below the average in terms of income, education and employment. At the same time, it ranked above the average in terms of age, numbers of single-parent families and numbers of people receiving various social and family benefits. Fifty percent of the adult population did not have a high school diploma, and many people had fewer than eight years of formal schooling. This demographic picture suggested a substantial need for literacy services dedicated to helping people enhance their educational achievement. However, the number of people accessing the services of the literacy program was small and had been declining over the previous few years. While the local college provided full-time adult upgrading and basic education starting at the Grade 4 level, it no longer offered classes at the Grades 1 to 3 levels.

As a literacy co-ordinator, I felt the need to find out why people were not using the literacy service available to them, given the demographic description of the community. I wondered if a different type of needs assessment would provide more useful information. Perhaps I could find out what kind of service was needed by contacting potential students and surveying them directly. I felt I should ask where in their lives a lack of literacy skills had stopped them from doing what they wanted to do independently. Having identified a need, I would ask them what they thought would be the best way to address it.

I decided to invite a number of Literacy and ABE students in programs at that time to form a group that would design and carry out a community needs assessment. I anticipated that adults who had experienced a need for more education and returned to school could draw on that experience, as well as on their knowledge of the community, to create a vehicle for discovering the needs felt by potential adult students. I also thought they would be able to contact people they knew who might be willing to talk about learning needs.

I hoped that the group's ideas would help me to provide a more useful literacy service in the community. The question that guided my research was, "What ideas would a group of students come up with in relation to conducting a needs assessment?"

Forming a Group

To form a group, I approached students from the literacy program and students who were enrolled in an adult upgrading class at the local college. I decided to approach upgrading students because they had made a public commitment to schooling. Also, there were very few students in the literacy program to draw from.

My first step was to visit staff at the local college and explain my needs assessment project to them. One of the instructors agreed to ask her basic education class if anyone would be interested in volunteering to help me. Three people from her class agreed to become involved. They came from different backgrounds and had a range of literacy levels, but they all had long-term goals that required high school completion.

Lily was a community health worker in her fifties who had taken a year off work to upgrade her math and science in order to enter a nursing course. Lily had approached the literacy program the previous year but found that work and family responsibilities did not leave her with enough time to study. She had decided to take a leave from work to attend the college full-time.

Charlene, age 19, wanted to finish her high school diploma. Miles, in his twenties, wanted to pursue a career in graphic arts. In order to go to art college he needed to complete high school. One student from the literacy program also agreed to join the group. Calvin, a 30 year-old, had been very active in promoting the program and had acted as a student representative for many years.

Gathering Information

I decided to tape-record the meetings with the students, log the meetings, and keep field notes. At the first meeting we talked about my idea for the needs assessment project. I explained the related research project and asked students for their permission to gather information from them and share it with others. The students signed consent forms agreeing to the use of their first names in reports, to the tape-recording of the committee meetings and to the publishing of any information. We decided to meet the next week to work on a questionnaire for the needs assessment.

What Happened

I had decided to use *Doing It Right! A Needs Assessment Workbook* (Edmonton Social Planning Council, 1993) as a reference to frame our discussions. However, when we got down to work, it became apparent that the students felt the idea of a needs assessment was a waste of time. To them the need for literacy services was so self-evident that spending time trying to find out if there was a need was like doing a study to see "whether ketchup is red." They thought that if there were no participants it was because nobody knew that the literacy program existed. In other words, the problem was not the lack of an appropriate service but the lack of adequate promotion. I, however, was still stuck on the idea of developing a needs assessment, so we spent the first meeting developing a questionnaire.

By the second meeting I had capitulated and I began to listen to what the group was really saying. We spent that meeting generating several ideas for promoting the program. I still was not really convinced about this course of action because I had tried most of these means of promotion in the past with little evidence of success. However, the group generated the idea of setting up a display in the local mall as a way of taking information out to the community. They were very enthusiastic and in the third week they met and created the display.

Two of the students set up the display at the mall and staffed it for several hours. During that time they succeeded in approaching and talking to seven people about the literacy program. At our fourth meeting we talked about the idea of students promoting the program and what training they would need to become "Program Ambassadors."

Analysis

I transcribed the tapes from the four group meetings. Even though this was time-consuming it was useful, because it allowed me to be an observer rather than an active participant. I was able to step back and get an over-all impression of the meetings. Then I read through the transcripts several times and identified a number of themes. This is a very difficult process to describe. As I went through the transcripts and field notes the first time it became apparent to me that several ideas recurred. I grouped these ideas into four themes. Then I reread the transcripts and used different colours to highlight ideas related to each theme. I found that, as well as ideas for promotion, the group had actually provided an answer to my original question about non-participation.

Recurring themes about non-participation included painful memories associated with reading and writing and experiences in school, people "getting by," and readiness to change.

Reasons for Non-participation

Painful memories

Listening to the tapes and reviewing the transcripts made it clear to me that reading and writing can be associated with strong emotions for some people. Asking people about their learning needs around literacy skills can create very negative responses. As Miles put it:

> *It's a very touchy question because it hits on for me, school was really very horrible and I hated it and a lot of people that can't read hated school and if you ask if they want to go back to school instantly they come back with defensive posture.*

In studying non-participation in adult literacy education, other researchers have related early schooling and adult attitudes. Quigley (1997) notes:

> It seems clear from every angle of study—quantitative, qualitative, and theoretical—that schooling has a lifelong impact. For countless non-participating adults, that impact has been so extremely negative that resistance to schooling is a persisting element in their lives. (p. 197)

As well, the transcripts revealed that people felt that if they had little schooling, they would not be able to do well in a new learning situation. It is likely that the needs assessment group was resistant to the idea of asking people to identify their lack of skills because it might reawaken painful memories of failure, and instead they recommended that we concentrate on promoting the program.

People getting by

The group often mentioned that, by and large, people could get by because they could read the basics. That is, they coped with literacy needs in their lives if they had a minimum grounding in literacy. Miles said:

> *Most people did go through a little bit of school and learned the basics of reading and nobody forgets that, you get by definitely, it's not impossible. But when you run into things like complicated things to read or a book—I don't think so!*

Lily gave us an example of people getting by with some support from their community. She worked as a community health worker and related her experience with people who were newly diagnosed as diabetics:

> *A lot of them read very little and to follow their diet it was very hard for them. So I used to have to go and visit with the Elders and explain to them what that means and how much they are supposed to eat, they didn't know how to read the scale. And once they learned how to use those things they were pretty good at it. I just had to show them, watching me.*

We also talked about situations that members of the group might find difficult to deal with, using banking as an example. Here again, they demonstrated that they could get by with a little support. All four members of the group had bank cards and had learned to use them. However, they mostly did their banking in person and requested that the tellers fill in their forms.

The group thus echoed the findings from the International Adult Literacy Survey (*Reading the Future*, 1996) that found that a large segment of the population has enough basic skills to read simple text but runs into difficulties with complicated instructions or prose. Ziegahn (1992) reported:

> The majority [of those with low reading ability] are not in programs, but use what literacy skills they have in their everyday lives. When these skills prove insufficient, they rely upon social networks and their own creativity to communicate with the literate world. (p. 30)

People might just need brief interventions, as Lily mentioned, to help them cope with their situations. Only those individuals who wanted to make changes would seek further schooling.

Readiness to change

Another recurring theme was that people need to reach their own decision that furthering their education will be needed in order to reach a certain goal. Until people have found a reason for change, no outside prodding will help. This is how Charlene said it:

> *I know quite a few people that dropped out of school Grade nine, ten, eleven, and want to go back to school but they don't have a clue about where they want to start. I can throw suggestions but it's really hard to register people that are really stubborn, set in their own ways.*

And Miles talked about his decision to return to school:

> *For three years I had the attitude I don't need that and basically I taught myself but now I'm at the point is where I've taught myself all I can and I need to get to school because I don't have credentials to do graphic arts, but I need my high school in order to get it.*

Program Promotion

The group felt it was very important that the program be visible and accessible. Once people realized that they would like to make a change, they needed to know where they could find help. Although the decision would ultimately rest with the individual, the group felt that active students could serve as role models for those contemplating change. Calvin said that, "people should know that adults can go back to school too." Lily echoed that thought:

> *The people when they ask me what I'm doing I tell them I'm back in school and they don't believe me, they ask me how old are you, and why, and then they say well if you can do it maybe I can.*

The group came up with the idea of students acting as Program Ambassadors to promote the literacy program. Students would serve as role models for others thinking about returning to school. To be effective, they would require training. They could design displays, posters, and brochures, and be equipped with program brochures and business cards.

Ideas for program promotion included:

- Be seen everywhere, participate in community events.

- Use posters that are short, simple, easy to see, easy to read. (Students suggested using ABC Canada's "We can help you with your reading, writing, math.")

- Put posters everywhere: bars, restaurants, grocery stores, the arena, swimming pool, bingo hall.

- Make displays colourful, simple, easy to read.

- Use word of mouth, use students as "ambassadors for the program" as role models.

- Emphasize that the program is flexible, easily accessible, tailored to individual's needs.

- Use TV and radio.

- Mention that math instruction is available, as well as reading and writing.

What I Learned from Doing This Project

I had started out with a set idea in mind—to do a needs assessment—and I had been intent on pursuing it. It was not until the third meeting that I finally heard what the group was telling me. Even then, I was not really convinced because I had tried most of the ideas for program promotion. It was not until I had finished the analysis and had some time to think about the project that I realized that my bedrock belief in the value of schooling and education was at odds with the group's experience. Their experience of school was negative, and they associated reading and writing with school. To approach people with questions about their needs (in other words, about their deficits) would automatically bring forth a negative emotional response.

Instead, the group wisely suggested that literacy programs establish themselves as part of the community. Students acting as program ambassadors could promote trust in the organization by speaking about their experiences with learning and emphasizing the flexibility and relevancy of the program. They would let potential students know they would have a say in choosing how and what to learn, and in setting their own goals.

Programs could also provide brief interventions for people who are not interested in making wholesale change but who might need extra support from time to time. For example, when speaking to potential participants I now mention that we are available if someone has difficulty filling in forms, or reading documents.

In terms of participatory practice it is not enough to just ask students for their input; we need to set aside our preconceived ideas and learn to listen. Quigley (1997) describes the prevailing attitude:

> Neither the schools nor the adult literacy world seems to hear this voice [of adult resisters]. When it is assumed that no one will listen, nothing is said. When nothing is said, nothing changes. (p. 203)

As practitioners, we need to make every effort possible to hear the voices of program participants.

References

Edmonton Social Planning Council. (1993). *Doing it right: A needs assessment workbook*. Edmonton, AB.

Reading the future: A portrait of literacy in Canada. A report on the International Adult Literacy Survey (IALS). (1996). Ottawa, ON: Government of Canada.

Quigley, B. A. (1997). *Rethinking literacy education: The critical need for practice-based change*. San Francisco: Jossey-Bass.

Ziegahn, L. (1992). Learning, literacy, and participation: Sorting out priorities. *Adult Education Quarterly, 43*, 30–50.

Chapter 10

Reflections

Grace Malicky[1]

---

[1]As with the introductory chapters in this book, Mary and I discussed content and reviewed and responded to each others' drafts. Although written by me, this chapter reflects our shared views.

Reflections

Individual researchers shared what they learned in each of the research reports in this volume. Mary and I met periodically throughout the project to reflect and talk about our learnings and the insights provided by the other researchers. In this final chapter, I will share some of our reflections relating to both participatory approaches and research in practice. I will conclude by presenting information on some ongoing activities that build on the Participatory Approaches in Adult Literacy Education/Research in Practice Project.

On Participatory Approaches

While the results of the individual research projects presented in this volume are not generalizable, combining results across projects suggests some common patterns. First, the researchers had little difficulty in locating people who were willing to become involved in participatory approaches projects. From these results, it is clear that some adults in literacy programs were not only willing to share power with project facilitators but, in some instances, went well beyond the expectations of these facilitators (see, for example, chapters by Linda and Veronica).

In every participatory approaches project, there were changes in the facilitators and learners. In some cases it was the relationships between the facilitators and learners that changed. These changes were to a large extent localized within the projects, but in some instances, extended well beyond the boundaries of specific projects. Perhaps the best example is from the project reported by Deborah. After this project was completed, Deborah and two other members of the writing group developed a proposal to attend and make a presentation at a national literacy and health conference in Ottawa. When health problems prevented Deborah from attending the conference, the other two women went to Ottawa and made the presentation on their own. It is unlikely that these women would have demonstrated this degree of empowerment before being involved in their participatory approaches project.

There was also evidence in nearly all of the research reports that facilitators faced challenges in adjusting their roles in a participatory context. Mary and Deborah focused their research on their roles and documented the struggles they and the other group members had with sharing power and control. However, Mary and Deborah were not the only facilitators who faced difficulties sharing power and creating safe authentic contexts for other individuals to share control of the operation and direction of projects. Adult literacy educators in other contexts who attempt to establish more egalitarian relationships with their students will find the frank discussion of struggles and difficulties in this volume to be of considerable assistance and comfort.

On Research in Practice

The participatory approaches projects clearly showed that adult learners can and will share power with adult educators given opportunity and support. The chapters presented in this volume also provide evidence that adult educators can and will engage in research, given opportunity and support. Indeed, I argue that many adult educators in the PAALE/RiP project not only *did* research but that they *became* researchers.

Becoming Researchers

It may be that some researchers involved in this project completed their research reports primarily because of a commitment Mary and I had made to agencies that funded the project. It was the involvement of these researchers in other activities, many beyond the requirements of the project, that revealed a change in identity from teacher or educator to teacher/researcher. In Fall 1998, Audrey, Andrea, Veronica and Mary attended and made a presentation at the provincial literacy conference in Calgary, and I joined them to make another presentation at a Research Seminar in Vancouver. In March 2000, Andrea, Veronica and Mary presented a round table at the Eastern Regional Adult Education Research Conference in Pennsylvania, moving into the international research community. Andrea and Veronica not only developed their round table presentation but also indicated that they felt they "belonged there" and were able to critique other presentations at the conference.

The change in identity is even more evident when one considers changes in some participants' professional lives. Veronica continues to coordinate a community literacy program that is now delivering a family literacy program. The program model is being researched as part of a national demonstration project. Veronica's decision to become involved with the demonstration was influenced by her experience in the research in practice project. Veronica and Andrea are serving as research mentors in the follow-up research in practice project described near the end of this chapter. For Mary and Linda, the project served to reinforce rather than change their research identity. Linda has enrolled in a doctoral program, and Mary continues to play an active role in the Canadian adult literacy research in practice scene and is facilitating the follow-up research in practice project. I have retired from the University of Alberta and am currently completing work with graduate students and a research colleague. However, partly as a result of this project, six researchers have either grown into the research role or extended their research skills. Among other prospects, they are ready to take my place in adult literacy research as I move to other types of activities. Clearly, research in practice has considerable potential to meet the goal of the National Literacy Secretariat (1998), in its framework for enhancing adult literacy research in Canada, of increased research capacity in adult literacy.

Rethinking Roles

In addition to changes in identity of the participating teacher researchers, this project also forced Mary and I to rethink the role of facilitator in research in practice. Our struggle to work in a collaborative, non-hierarchical way with researchers paralleled that of participatory approaches facilitators as they attempted to share power and control with the participants in their projects. In order to empower teacher-researchers, we felt that it was crucial to establish egalitarian relationships and provide assistance rather than direction. Resources on research were provided for participants to use on an as-needed basis. Individual and group meetings were scheduled to discuss progress on research and answer questions, but we tried not to tell individual researchers what to do.

From the results of an independent evaluation of the overall project completed by Yvon Laberge (2000), it appears that we achieved only partial success in our attempt to establish collaborative, egalitarian relationships through modeling rather than direct instruction. Some researchers indicated that at times they didn't know what to ask in order to get the help they needed. Others indicated that they felt they were somehow expected to fit into a structure but that this structure was never communicated to them. In spite of our assurances that we valued diversity, individual researchers questioned if they were doing things the "right" way.

Our struggle to achieve collaborative relationships was accentuated when it came time to produce the written product. Our dilemma was this. If we provided a high degree of structure for these final reports, we risked losing the voices of individual researchers and decreasing their sense of identity as researchers. If we provided no structure, we risked losing credibility with established academics. We were also torn between two potential audiences—adult literacy educators and university-based academics. Was our major goal to encourage other literacy educators to venture into the unfamiliar terrain of research in practice? Or were we primarily intent on convincing academics that research in practice has a legitimate place alongside their research? By deciding to do both, we placed a heavy burden on researchers, most of whom were writing their first formal research report. Working with researchers to revise and complete the papers in this volume provided us with our greatest struggle and our harshest criticism from participants. One individual commented in the evaluation undertaken by Yvon that by the end of the process, she felt that the final product was more ours than hers. It is clear now that we needed to address the questions of purposes and audiences more directly at the beginning of the writing process and to discuss our dilemma with individual researchers during the process itself.

Introducing Research in Practice to Educators

Overall, a major goal of this project was for adult literacy educators to become researchers by engaging in the research process with our support. All of the individuals involved met this goal. Some of the comments provided to Yvon in the evaluation included: "I . . . know now that research is not something I need to be afraid of." "I also learned that I am quite capable of doing research." However, this learning-by-doing way of introducing educators to research in practice was not without problems. One of the challenges involved the broad scope of many research projects, which resulted in the collection of large amounts of data. Learning to do analysis, while doing it with large amounts and varied sources of data, was daunting and took more time than anticipated. Another challenge was presented by the reference materials I provided on research methods. According to Yvon's report, some participants found these materials too difficult. At least part of the problem was lack of familiarity with the vocabulary of educational research.

In a paper prepared for the National Literacy Secretariat, Jenny Horsman and Mary Norton (1999) propose an alternative model for introducing practitioners to research in practice. They recommend engaging practitioners in the following activities:

- learning about and from research
- reflecting on research and its implications for practice
- using research to develop daily practice
- doing research about practices.

Jenny and Mary also advocate a coordinated system of support for research in practice. All of the participants in the research reported in this volume underlined how crucial support was to their involvement. They could not have worked full time and completed their research without both financial support and research assistance. The ideas in Jenny and Mary's paper, as well as what we learned from our experiences in the PAALE/RiP project, have been incorporated into the follow-up project described below.

What Next?

This volume demonstrates some of the potential of research in practice to contribute to knowledge and practice in adult literacy education. We hope that it will serve as both a stimulus for further research in practice by other teams of researchers and as one model for this type of research. By reporting both our successes and struggles, we also hope that future researchers will be able to take advantage of what we learned about research in practice.

As indicated above, most of the participants in this project continue to be involved in research in some capacity. In addition, the National Literacy Secretariat has funded a follow-up project sponsored by the Literacy Coordinators of Alberta that involves collaboration of individuals from that organization, The Learning Centre Literacy Association and the Centre for Research on Literacy at the University of Alberta. The major purpose of this project is to develop a collaborative network to support adult literacy practitioners engaging in research in practice and to build links among field-based and university-based practitioners and researchers. The project will also build and share knowledge about research in practice through project evaluation, linking with similar networks, publishing information from the network, and organizing a Research in Practice Gathering.

Part of this new project included provision of a university credit course entitled Introduction to Research in Practice in Adult Literacy, which was offered for the first time in Fall 2000. This course began with reading and learning about research in practice before involving educators in doing research. This format will hopefully ease the entry of practitioners into research in practice.

We believe that the key to increased research in practice is the synergy that develops when field-based and university-based researchers and practitioners come together to learn more about adult literacy education. It is this collaboration that will sustain future efforts and produce the quality research needed to inform policy and improve the practice of adult literacy education in Canada.

References

Horsman, J., & Norton, M. (February, 1999). A framework to encourage and support practitioner involvement in adult literacy research in practice in Canada. A paper prepared for the National Literacy Secretariat.

Laberge, Y. (August, 2000). Participatory approaches in adult literacy education/Research in Practice Project. Evaluation Report.

Literacy Coordinators of Alberta. (June, 2000). Research in practice in adult literacy networks. Project Proposal submitted to the National Literacy Secretariat.

National Literacy Secretariat. (1998). *Enhancing literacy research in Canada*. Ottawa: Human Resources Development Canada.